THE LAND
of
LOST LOGIC

Janette Mostert

authorHOUSE®

AuthorHouse™
1663 Liberty Drive
Bloomington, IN 47403
www.authorhouse.com
Phone: 1-800-839-8640

I have tried to recreate events, locales and conversations from my memories of them. In order to maintain their anonymity in some instances I have changed the names of individuals and places, I may have changed some identifying characteristics and details such as physical properties, occupations and places of residence.

Published by AuthorHouse   10/10/2012

ISBN: 978-1-4772-1510-4 (sc)
ISBN: 978-1-4772-1511-1 (e)

This is for my family, Col and Tim,
John, Mum, Jacqui and Jo &
in memory of dad & Nanny.

Contents

ACKNOWLEDGEMENTS

MY LOVE AND thanks to Colin and Tim, for all their encouragement. My family; mum, John, Jacqui and Jo for theirs.

My brother, John Crowley, Glenys Crowly and Michele Bowes whose combined efforts in the editing and advice department made all the difference! And lastly to all the friends I made in Saudi—Especially Delia Hardcastle and the rest—you know who you are.

INTRODUCTION

SAUDI ARABIA IS not an easy country to enter, this is because the kingdom only grants tourist visas to visitors who are part of a tour group rather than the individual tourist or backpackers, who are generally not allowed to pop in and have a look around (at least not without tons of paperwork and red tape and who needs that, right!)

Nor does it get any easier once you have been given permission to enter for a longer period of time.

Western women who live and work in Saudi are restricted to those with specific professional qualifications, experience and skills such as nurses, teachers and secretaries. Those who don't work have come into Arabia with their husbands.

A lot has been written about the country from different perspectives. This book is about my experiences as a western woman, married, but on a single contract with a husband and small son who were both on my husband's 'married' contract, which did in fact include me, but not as far as my work permit was concerned! To mix things up a little, the hospital I worked for, as a Nursing Supervisor in the Education department of a military hospital, was around forty kilometers away from the hospital my husband worked at, which co-incidentally was also the living compound for the three of us.

Unfortunately I did not have opportunity to meet and mingle with many Saudi locals—mainly due to the strict Islamic laws, which meant meeting the ordinary Saudi woman was difficult. Working in a hospital environment made it all the more challenging as my experiences are based mostly on communication with staff rather than the patients.

It is a complex society, whose laws do not lend itself to western ideology or traditions—and why should they. That's what makes the country such a strangely fascinating place to Westerners. Written initially as a personal diary, I have put together my experiences and observations of the Saudi system within the environment I found myself. I didn't go 'native' and spend months in the desert with the Bedouin, though that would have been interesting! This book is therefore not intended to be anything more than a personal account of the two years I spent in this fascinating land that was at once, strange, infuriating, exciting, endearing, exasperating but never was it dull!

Marhuba!

Janette Mostert
Cape Town 2012

CHAPTER ONE

"All journeys have secret destinations of which the traveler is unaware."

Martin Buber

Getting there . . .

WADING THROUGH THICK black mud, I slowly urge my weary body through the viscous mixture. Gazing down, I'm startled to note that I'm wearing a long dark coat that covers my body from shoulder to feet, and try to rationalize my choice of headgear—a large black fedora—which is now attempting to block my view. All around me is sand, mounds and mounds of the stuff. A deep golden colour, it slowly envelops me, its aureate grains lodge in my eyes, nose and throat. I'm desperately fighting for air as the sand constricts my every pore.

I awake, gasping for breath. Everything is still for a few minutes save my heart beating wildly.

The pillow slides off my face as I squint over at the light curtains drawn closed to the cold July morning; I recall now where I am. It's Bethlehem, the African one, South Africa to be exact. Anyway there's no bright star, three wise men or beds of straw.

I yawn luxuriously and flex my arms. The moment has finally come—we're off to that dark and mysterious place in the North: Saudi Arabia. Joining Colin who has already been there for six months and by all accounts is turning into a camel! This Bethlehem is freezing. Although we are on the same longitude our latitude in the Southern hemisphere puts us right in the middle of a chilly winter in contrast to the oven-like heat I will soon experience up North.

Hobbling over to the bathroom, icy water startles my face out of its somnolence simultaneously tightening my pores. I dress quickly. First the loose, dark cloak-like garment called an *abaya*, which closes off my body from view. I toy with the dark *niqab* (head and face cover and veil) that shuts off my features altogether then feeling ridiculous, I keep only the head scarf on and throw the rest into my large handbag. I'll be wearing it long enough when we get to Saudi.

Thoughts dash around my head like flies around a cowpat. Saudi Arabia. It still sounds mysterious even after months of speaking the name—mostly cursing it—as the procedure for applying to work there takes ever longer and longer. What with filling in and posting copious amounts of paperwork—proof of birth and marriage, police clearance, qualifications and references and naturally proof of robust health is mandatory. It seemed that we would never actually get there.

I waken Tim and help him into his clothes (luckily as a male and a six year old child to boot, his clothing restrictions are non existent, in sharp contrast to mine.)

"You look funny mummy," he says gazing at me with some alarm.

"You'd better get used to it Tim," I snap, "Mummy's going to look 'funny' for a while!"

"Here you are sis, er I mean *bint*" Jacqui smiles and passes me a mug of steaming tea.

I take it and snarl fondly at her.

"Let's have brekky at the airport. God, I can't imagine what the whole thing will be like!"

"Hmm. Well, it'll be an adventure I guess,"

"Just wish I was more confident about the whole 'being a woman in Saudi' thing." I hyphenate with my fingers.

"You *are* a woman, a Westerner and there's nothing you can do about it." Jacqui, the practical member of the family, removes the tea things and says we have to get going. The airport is a few hours away.

Sally, my recruitment representative arrives at the appointed hour, a pleasant plump girl with a shock of blond hair and intense brown eyes. She hugs me, stands back a little and exclaims,

"Wow, you really look the part!"

"You don't think it's all a bit much?"

She reassures me with a little pat while helping to push the trolley towards the check-in counter. There's a flurried exchange of papers, passports, tickets and forms. Sally provides information in short bursts,

"Now keep calm" she begins, "don't let them get you angry and remember not to be rude—they hate that."

She adds somewhat enigmatically,

"Expect delays, abruptness and to be chucked into a room by the *Muttawan*."

"The religious police." she adds noting my puzzled expression.

I reassure her I'll be fine but seriously begin to doubt it! Even Jacqui starts to look worried at this last minute's rapid exchange of advice. A quick hug and Sally leaves me to ponder her words. I rearrange the long veil over my head, and we wander off in search of tea. There's a restaurant nearby and the three of us place our order (both tea *and* coffee for me for some reason I can't at this moment fathom). With some interested stares at my Islamic garb, I defiantly order a large ham and cheese sandwich. It may be the last bit of ham I'll have for some time I think with some alarm. Jacqui stares at me for a minute while I sip my tea holding the veil raised between two fingers.

"Do you have to wear that thing over your face?" She asks.

"The *naqib*? Yup, I read it in the 'Westerners guide to Saudi Arabia', it's a strict Islamic country you know!"

In fact Westerners are not obliged to wear the full-face cover but I only find that out much later. For the moment I look an absolute *eedjit* in my ignorance. A month or so ago I entered an Islamic clothing store in Cape Town and chose a *white naqib* instead of the more traditional black. This white cloth now lies like a melting ice cream on my head against the dark material of the *abaya.*

After swallowing the meal in haste, I can no longer bear the wait for the boarding call to be announced, so we check in early, leaving a worried looking Jacqui gazing after us from behind the partition. She gives a last quick wave as we shuffle out of view through to customs. My hand luggage weighs a ton and the money belt around my waist keeps sliding round to nestle in the small of my back resulting in an unsightly sacral lump.

"Please fasten your seatbelt." smiles the svelte Saudia flight attendant as she passes by. She wears a tailored royal blue uniform with gold braiding, matching hat and scarf that covers her hair. She manages to look both elegant and smart whilst remaining within the cultural boundaries for dress. As we taxi slowly along the runway I note with interest that the TV attached to the seat in front of me has an arrow to the left of the screen. This is for those who wish to prostrate themselves for prayer, in the direction of Mecca, during the flight. Airlines such as this one have dedicated prayer rooms in their long-haul aircraft. Most of the airlines have them in the rear of the cabin (between galley and cabin). In fact prayers may be performed while seated if necessary.

After take off we are issued with thin blue blankets and marshmallow sized pillows. Tim and I cover our knees and settle into our seats to watch a movie until dinner is served—children first. I'm dying for a glass of wine but settle for some orange juice, seeing as I'm not about to get anything remotely alcoholic for some time to come. I try not to allow this to affect me too much having recently become rather fond of a glass or two of the fermented grape with dinner. Oh all right, it's not recent and not always just with dinner either!

My attention draws to the meal itself, which is rather tasty; lamb meatballs and fragrant rice. Tim has fish pieces—in the shape of small fish!

Although it is hajj time the plane isn't overly full. There are only a few Westerners, the rest, mostly Indians, Filipino's and some South Africans of Moslem faith. A few hours later, a trip to the toilet reveals bidet facilities, unisex perfume and a luxurious hand cream and aftershave. I smother myself in all three, which sets the tone a bit and walk back with that slightly halting gait that flying affords while smelling like a Parisian perfume counter.

The small TV screen flashes and flickers; a BBC cookery program is in progress;

> *'Take your Monk fish, olive oil, sun dried tomatoes and anchovies rolled in flour and herbs and bake for 25minutes at 180 degrees C,' gushes a stiff haired blonde holding up her tray of baked fish as proof of her baking capabilities.*

Sighing a little, I move my marshmallow to the side of my head and attempt to nod off. I can never sleep on planes and tonight is no exception.

We land around 06:45 pm and I grope around for all the hand luggage, nervously straightening my *abaya* and pulling the veil over my head. Taking a deep breath and holding Tim tightly with one hand and several pieces of luggage in the other, we disembark.

Diary excerpt:

> *Col has organized someone to pick us up and take us to a hotel in Jeddah overnight. We will fly onto Al-Khyber to join him later. Wonder what the whole thing is going to be like?*

The bus jerks to a halt outside the large open doorway of the airport building and passengers climb from the cool interior into air with the humidity of a hot damp sponge. Tim is given another colourful bag containing sunglasses, a hat, a book and some oranges by the smiling flight attendant and he clutches this tightly to his chest. He looks slowly around him.

"Wow! It's very hot," he observes flicking limp strands of hair off his forehead.

"Daddy didn't tell us it's going to be so hot," he continues looking annoyed at this omission. I squeeze his small hand reassuringly,

"Don't worry Tim."

More for my benefit than his I add,

"We'll get used to it and then we'll have some fun!"

Ah, famous last words! It wasn't fun. Not even a little. It was to be almost twenty-four hours of hell for me.

Damn it! I can hardly see through my veil. My eyes, misting over in the heat, take some moments to adjust.

Where to go? Two options exist: 'transit' or 'Saudi immigrants'. I'm not sure either option applies to us. In fact *we* are to leave the airport altogether with some friend of Colin's and go to a nice cool air-conditioned hotel till the morning when we will wake up to soft Arabian music, a typical Middle Eastern breakfast before flying on to Al-Khyber.

Perking up at the thought, I look around wondering where the man who is to pick us up from the airport will be waiting.

"How will I recognize him, or he me?" I wonder tucking my veil firmly over my head and choosing a long queue consisting of mostly Arab and Indians.

I settle Tim on the trolley in front of me and stand waiting. Perspiration trickles down my armpits into the waistband of the money belt. Feeling very uncomfortable in the prickly hot *abaya* and veil, I suddenly feel panicky. No one will know I'm a Western woman! I quickly remove the gauze covering my face and peer around, blinking sweat out of my eyes. My gaze falls on Tim's prostrate form and I have to smile—he is a carbon copy of Col. Thus reassured, I replace the *niqab* over my face and inch forward.

Looking around, I notice most of the men in the queue are wearing white toweling around their midriffs and very little else. I later learn that this is the type of clothing worn by first timers to the hajj. The garments consist of one piece of cloth (called *izar*) that is wrapped around the middle to cover the body from their stomach to mid-calves or lower; the other (called *rida*) is draped around the pilgrim's shoulders to cover the upper body. The whole gives a faint air of ridicule as hairy grown men parade around in what amounts to nothing more than a bath towel.

The wait seems interminable and by midnight the queue hasn't moved more than a few steps. No one can tell me why. It has already been hours of travelling, seven of them standing in the airport without anything to drink or anyone to speak to.

I am rather anxious to get to the other side of the carousel and find the person that is supposed to be taking us to a hotel. The night is rapidly coming to an end—it's unlikely he will want to wait around forever. In fact he probably hasn't! Who to ask? I've read recently that I mustn't speak to any male who is not my husband. There are only a handful of females around and they are all local women who silently allow their male members of family manage the process. A few Pakistani child minders hold sleeping children or push prams. We move forward another step and wait. It appears what westerners there were have already left.

Around 2:30 a.m. a thin, veiled woman comes up to me and says,

"سايك أبل ج يتأت". Well, what she's really saying is, "*come to bring bags*."

Dutifully, I follow her past the still flowing queues to the room behind where our luggage is waiting. She disappears as quickly as she arrived and I set about looking for my suitcases. Two of them lie unattended next to the now still carousel. Where's the other one? Ah there it is! lying underneath a swarthy bearded man's suitcase. Hang on! He's wheeling it away on a trolley! A piece of vibrant red string tied to the side handle immediately identifies it as mine, as well as the fact that it's a particularly large flowery one.

"Hey!" I shout, staggering after him, impeded by the abaya. He continues walking, deliberately ignoring me. All the pent up anger from the preceding few hours is unleashed.

"Stop you thief! That is *my* suitcase!"

If there's one word you do not utter too loudly in Saudi it is the word 'thief'. Some orange-jacketed officials look up at the commotion. The bearded man stops and holds up a large meaty hand,

"Sorry lady, it was lying unattended and I was taking it to the authorities."

I stare at him in disbelief. He is wheeling the thing towards the open doors that lead outside! I grab the handle, sending his suitcase tumbling to the floor. He snatches it up and hurries off glancing around anxiously in case this exchange had been noted. It has, but the yellow jackets are choosing to ignore us. As a woman it's not worth causing a stir.

Tears of self pity prick at my eyelids, I'm hot, tired, dressed up like a Jedi knight, no-one is telling me anything and I'm too scared to speak to anyone in case I'm breaking some strict Saudi law.

What has happened to the nice man who is to take us to a hotel? Soft beds, cool sheets, hot tea. My lip trembles. Col can't even be contacted to hear to what has happened.

"Open now!"

The stony-faced customs official standing next to his steel table doesn't seem at all friendly. He wants me to open my suitcase. A stash of magazines is nestled in under my dainties for later consumption. I'm not sure he will like them. They have photographs of women's bare arms. A gesture towards the lock informs him it is broken.

"My things will fall out if you open my case!"

He ignores me and pokes around my clothes and undergarments in full view of everyone else in the queue. I have a fleeting wish I'd packed a side of bacon in there so that we'd be sent home!

"Go!" he announces curtly, finding nothing to declare.

An apparition in black suddenly appears genie-like in front of my chair screeching something unintelligible. She's shaking a black-gloved finger at me. Not knowing the nature of my transgression, I just look back at her in bewilderment. She doesn't like me looking at her and this releases another torrent of Arabic. She continues to shake her finger under my nose.

I could bite it but I'm a little frightened of her. My passport is removed from me and taken away by the nasty harridan. I worry if I'll ever see it again. My querulous query brings nothing more than a shrug.

Diary excerpt:

It is way after 3am. Have long ago given up on a hotel. Guess we just hang around until the plane that flies on to Al-Khyber arrives. No idea when that will be—why would I! Nothing to do but try and get some sleep. Not sure how easy that is going to be as the loudspeaker goes off every twenty minutes or so, the lights are blazing and the wall behind us appears to be a thinly partitioned prayer room. I've just realized how easy it is to show the soles of your feet to other people and that is a strict no-no here, an offence of disrespect. I have been 'disrespectful' at least three times in half an hour!

After much tossing and turning I just manage to get into a position with a modicum of comfort when suddenly the 'Darth Vader's' appear and shout,

"Wake up! Wake up! We go now!"

Hastily trying to fight sleep and bewilderment at this sudden burst of activity, I gather both my wits and Tim and scrabble to my feet following everyone through a door leading outside.

The air is, even at this early hour, hot and humid. Filipina nurses line up lethargically in front of a waiting airport bus. By now I am used to the fact that no one explains anything and resign myself to discovering the next move in stages. We just stand and wait.

Thirty minutes of stifling inactivity follow and then we are ushered onto the bus. It has been nearly twenty four hours of travelling. We are driven around the huge airport and deposited at some other terminal. At least there are a few plastic seats to sit on. Tim is thankfully still sleeping.

Hearing a familiar sound I turn to find a blonde haired girl near a check-in counter screaming abuse (in Afrikaans!) at a bored looking Saudi official.

"Julle's n klomp dom mense! Se net waar's my bleddie vliegtuig!"

It appears she has come in from Bahrain at 6am this morning and is asking (none too politely) where her plane is. The lack of concern or response from the official alerts me to the notion that I had best keep calm and respectful if I am to get anywhere and especially out of this airport. I'd like to speak with this girl and ask her a million questions but she disappears around the corner.

And so begins another interminable wait on hard seats, my eyes red and gritty from lack of sleep. Tim in youthful contrast is now wide awake and playing around the seats, running up and down the long shiny tiled floor of the airport lounge.

Resigning myself to staying awake till the call to board the next plane comes; I survey the hall and try not to think about how long we may have to remain here before anyone notices us missing!

It just doesn't bear thinking about—so I don't!

A kindly local man in a brown *thobe* opens his shop for the day and sends over a Coke for Tim. This small act of kindness causes my lip to tremble again with raw emotion as he gestures the drink is for Tim. He asks by way of a drinking motion whether I'd also like a drink and in five minutes I am sipping pure nectar! Actually it's sugarless tea and frothy milk in a disposable cup but tastes delicious. He has saved my sanity and I beam my thanks. Pity he can't see it through the veil!

The call eventually comes through around 8:30 am. An hour or two later we're climbing down the mobile steps at Al-Khyber's airport in the North Eastern province.

Tim, myself and another South African nurse are whisked away from the others onto a separate bus by the surly official who true to form, decides it isn't worth parting any information to mere women. This *segregation extremis* is beginning to unnerve me.

After half an hour of sitting in silence I venture a few questions to my South African companion. She is dressed in a black *abaya* but her hair is uncovered. She says she is going to work at a large hospital near Jeddah. It is her first time as well and she appears as confused as I am as to the process. Eventually we are led into another room by some khaki clothed individual who asks who our sponsors are. At this stage I'm not even sure who I am! I mumble something about my husband waiting for us (again I'm not even sure this is true). I'm getting thoroughly fed up with the constant game of musical chairs. The South African girl is whisked away, presumably by her sponsor and Tim and I find ourselves alone in the huge hangar, wondering when this nightmare is going to end.

After some time, I hear a familiar voice. It's Colin. I see his silhouette against the entrance at the far end of the hangar. Tim jumps up and runs towards him shouting,

"Daddy, daddy!" at the top of his lungs. I feel tempted to do the same but only the thought that some Arabian official may be watching with disapproval at this 'typical female' behaviour stops me, instead I venture a,

"Hallo pet, where the hell were you!"

It is then that I notice another figure walking alongside Col. It is 'my sponsor' from the King Sayeed Military Hospital (KSMH)—a large bearded man in military uniform. I can't face another minute of Saudi Bureaucracy with a uniformed stranger and restrain myself from throwing my tired quivering body at Col's feet weeping in relief and try a greeting instead.

"This is your sponsor." Col informs me and I give him a weak smile. At this moment anyone even vaguely responsible for the events of the past twenty-four hours isn't going to see my best side. It occurs to me he can't see my face anyway so I scowl at him. Col speaks to another official who has suddenly appeared at my side from another door. My passport is produced and 'Mr. Sponsor' flicks his thumb through it quickly. I have lifted my veil, and although the woman in front of him barely resembles the photograph contained within, he appears satisfied. He does not return my passport. This will stay with the hospital authorities until my contract ends.

"You *weel* receive your *iqama* in due course." He promises, before striding off. An iqama, is similar to a green card in USA, only this is a small maroon booklet that allows one to live (or work) in Saudi Arabia for as long as you (or your husband) has a contract. You must have one if you are not a Saudi citizen. It accompanies your passport, which also requires an entrance/exit visa stamp. You may not work or travel around the kingdom without it. In fact, without an *iqama,* you can't open a bank account, take out loans, buy a car, or do most other things associated with settling down to reside in a new country. The employer is usually responsible for ensuring that an employee receives one.

For the time being I think he's just promised me a large lizard.

Unlike Westerners, returning to Saudi is easier for Arabian women. No one stops her or asks questions but if the woman does not hold a Saudi passport and does not have a *mahram*—a male relative accompanying her, then she is held at the airport until her sponsor, whether an employer or relative, comes to get her.

Colin and I are allowed to leave the humid confines of the airport hangar.

He glances at me as we round the corner,

"What the hell are you wearing all that stuff for?" he asks, nodding towards my covered head and face. I finger the veil defensively and mutter something about respecting the laws of the place.

"You don't have to wear the face mask." he chuckles leading us to a very smart looking silvery-gold Toyota land cruiser. I instinctively want to open the left hand door but Col reminds me,

"Other door, it's left hand drive here".

Colin seems a bit harassed and admits he has sneaked away from work and has to be back within the hour. He says I have to go through the motions of seeing my single residential quarters before we can go home. I'm on a single contract of course. I couldn't be less interested. The place we drive to is called the Corniche centre and is situated in the mid town area. It is around 42° C (107.6°F) and I'm finding all the rushing around in extreme temperatures after one hour's sleep, a bit much. Colin asks a uniformed man at the entrance to the Corniche Centre where the nurse's apartments are located and he points us in the right direction.

Up two flights of stairs and into a small reception room that smells of boiled cabbage.

"*Murhaba.*" he says haltingly and I suppress a snigger. Col was never much of a linguist and even this one word of greeting has been tortured beyond recognition.

"I come with my wife to collect her apartment key. She is Janette Mostert"

The short dark haired man behind a counter nods and removes an envelope from beneath the counter and presents me with my apartment key and an official letter from my hospital. Duty duly taken care of, we leave for King Waheed Military hospital (KWMH). This is where Colin works and where we live; an open hospital compound and a far cry from the usual Western compounds. This means in effect that once outside our front door, I have to remain covered up unlike western compounds where such restrictions are left at the gate.

I am struck by the incongruity of the smooth four-lane tar roads, which stretch out like thick black belts within the surrounding pale, undulating landscape. Modern technology amidst miles and miles of ancient white sand, interspersed with metal debris, the remains of cars, trucks and mangy camels.

Very quickly the 'rules' of the road become clear: First, there *are* no rules or apparent speed limits and a four-lane highway is easily turned into six lanes by virtue of bully tactics; shouldering your vehicle into any available space and simply increasing speed.

"Your hospital is about forty kilometers from our compound," explains Col,

"I'll have to work out how to get you there. Maybe you can use a taxi. You know you can't drive?" he glances at me quickly and I nod,

"Yeah, read all about *that* archaic law!"

Saudi Arabia is the only country in the world that prohibits women from driving.

When police recently spotted three Arabian women driving one night, they gave chase. The women speeded up to try and escape but their car collided with the police vehicle and they were all arrested. Women are banned from driving in the conservative Moslem kingdom but there has been a campaign by Saudi women over the past year to end the ban.[1]

Dr. Fahd Bin Abdul Kareem states that, '50% of the traffic accidents in the Kingdom are caused by women despite the fact they do not drive cars.' I saw this headline in the local paper after a month in the country and cut it out, shaking my head in disbelief. Luckily I can multitask.

In Saudi Arabia, women's driving has been a controversial issue since 1990. The Guardian reporter Eman Al Nafjan wrote on Tuesday 6 December 2011 that one Professor Kamal al-Subhi prepared a study on the effects of women driving on society. One of his observations revealed that:

---

[1] Quoted from Emirates 24/7 http://www.emirates247.com/ crime/region/three-women-arrested-for-driving-in-saudi- 2012-08-05-1.470208

"After a while, a woman got up and walked to her car in the parking lot in front of the Starbucks we were in. She shouted at the Indian cleaning her car for not doing a good job of it. She was wearing a pair of pants so tight that her innermost organs were discernible. Despite that, she put her hands on her knees and bowed down to point at a lower part of the car that the Indian had missed. The young men at the cafe were attentively watching through the glass at this undoubtedly arousing scene. The whole place was indecent and smelt of moral disintegration."

I muse that with views like this, the women here have no hope of driving anytime soon! For the moment however I am more than happy that Colin is driving as yet another large car zooms past my window, so close I can see he hasn't shaved this morning.

Tim, still clutching his bright Saudia Airways rucksack gazes quietly out of the window. We eventually arrive at gate One, the first of two before officially entering King Waheed Hospital in Al-Khyber. Colin is waved in after a cursory look at the license disc. As he turns into our section of the compound (the 'married quarters') he spies John and Nicci, our South African neighbours. The Maraises had taken Col under their collective wing while waiting for Tim and I to arrive. I smile a greeting and am dimly aware of some small talk. I am beyond polite chatter at this stage, almost paralyzed with tiredness. Colin leads us through glass doors into a small entrance lobby and then we are in our apartment.

Two things strike me, the size of the rooms (huge), and the awful colour scheme, (burnt orange and 'turd' brown). I turn to my husband, who is removing his beeper from his pocket,

"This is awful isn't it?"

He nods in agreement and strides into the lounge setting down the suitcases on a dark brown carpet. We're left to sort ourselves out while Col returns to work, about five minutes away in the main hospital building. Despite my tiredness I get my second wind and set about unpacking and setting out some things to make it all seem more homely. Tim selects his bedroom from the three on offer and bounces around on his bed of choice before unpacking his toys with abandon.

Having slept well for most of the day, I'm ready to do some shopping in the town of Al-Khyber. The heat is still intense and the driving terrible. Colin stops at an outside restaurant at the seafront for supper.

"If we're quick we will miss 2nd prayer."

Apparently if you manage to order food before prayer time you are allowed to continue eating after the muezzin has called the prayer, although it has to be done behind closed doors.

We sit outside, as it is cooler, in one of the sections allocated for married couples. There is a low table and some wooden benches, a dividing partition and a curtain between us and the other diners. We order a local meal consisting of flat, chewy *naan* type bread, known simply as Arabic bread, couscous, lamb kebabs, cucumber and yogurt from the white-jacketed Pakistani waiter.

My tea arrives in a pot with tinfoil in place of a lid! I take an appreciative sniff. Mmm, mint tea—very refreshing.

The family section is situated in a corner well away from the singles who eat inside or near the door, also curtained off. The place is overrun with feral cats, strange looking animals with smallish heads and very long thin bodies. They yowl and stretch besides us, hopeful for a *'stray'* morsel. We try to ignore them. A tall electric fan blows in a desultory manner throughout the meal but doesn't make much difference to the temperature, managing instead to blow all the paper napkins off the table.

CHAPTER TWO

The use of traveling is to regulate imagination by reality, and instead of thinking how things may be, to see them as they are."

Samuel Johnson

Settling in

I AM UP EARLY the next day for an appointment at the Nurse's centre. Not happy about leaving Tim behind in the apartment but I have no choice. Col says he'll pop in as often as he can. He orders a taxi to come and pick me up. It arrives late. A Pakistani driver hastily ushers me into the back seat more for reasons of legality than chivalry.

We arrive at the Corniche centre and I fumble with some twenty Riyal notes with uncertainty then can't remember which of the many entrances the right one is. Is it okay to ask the male doorman? Darn nuisance trying to work out this Islamic cultural business, how do I guess what is correct and what isn't without offending anyone! I eventually ask the doorman anyway. He leads me silently inside and up the stairs to a room with a counter against one side. A small dark haired woman enters the room and introduces herself as the housing secretary. She is Filipina. I'm led into another small room which contains a handful of recruits, both male and female and all Filipino.

Filipinos first arrived in Saudi Arabia in 1973, when a group of Filipino engineers migrated to the country The inclusion of nurses and male workers many years later has brought the numbers of Filipinos to over a million at present but a small percentage only are Moslem. Roman Catholicism is the predominant religion in the Philippines and is the largest Christian denomination. Filipina trained nurses form most of the 'western' complement in many hospitals in Saudi.

An Arab male comes in and sits down in front of me. At first I don't recognize him but it turns out he's the same hospital representative who had come to the airport with Col. He and I are offered something to drink but not the Filipino recruits. I'm told later that this is more in deference to my senior position than racial segregation. I'm not totally convinced. My tea arrives black and sweet. I don't tell them I prefer it milky and sugarless and sip tentatively waiting to see what happens next. The tiny round-faced Filipina housekeeper proceeds to go through some ground rules with regard to living at the Corniche centre, which includes such pointers as:

"You no go out after curfew." She pronounces it '*kerfoo*.'

"Filipina who do that, go home on next plane!" And, with an emphatic shake of her head,

"No bad tings to happen in room. It *happen*, you go home on plane." She neglects to mention what the 'bad tings' could be but I think we all get the idea. I speak to the hospital rep and he says I am to start work on the 3rd July. After some minutes form filling I am shown to my apartment and left there to contemplate my fate.

My single nurse's apartment consists of two bedrooms sparsely furnished and a small lounge and kitchenette. None of it appears very homely and in fact is rather depressing, dark and dreary, and the apartment smells of wet carpet. Can't believe the difference between our apartment at King Waheed and this one for the nurses. I am apparently 'sharing' this apartment with another South African girl who is also married but on a single contract as she is here alone, her family still in South Africa. I don't think either of us will use it much. I later try and give up the room citing 'other accommodation available' but this is vetoed and I'm told to keep it.

"Hi pet," I nestle the phone under my chin and turn to look at my reflection in the small bedside mirror, and grimace. I look like another six hours sleep might help to rearrange my puffy sleep deprived face into something more human and less 'Pilsbury man'.

"Can you fetch me at about 10? This place is awful!"

I decide to visit the library while I'm waiting. It appears to have been stocked with paperbacks from previous inhabitants. Mainly bad romances if the covers are anything to go by. According to the rules (typed neatly against the library wall) you merely choose what you want to read and if possible replace the book with one of your own. I pick up a novel with a peeling spine; *Passionate interlude* exclaims its lurid title. The cover photograph has a woman leaning against a tree. A tall handsome man leans towards her with pursed lips as if to steal a kiss. What amuses me is that she appears to be wearing an *abaya*. The *Mattawan* have ensured the object of passion is fully clothed and showing not an inch of bare skin! Where a heaving bosom would surely have been is now a thick dark smudge of felt tip pen, indelible and censorious. I choose something about travelling through India on a bicycle instead.

It is time to wait in the reception area for Col and Tim to arrive. Colin tells me he has bought a satellite dish but it needs connecting. The sooner the better as local stuff is riveting (not!)

This afternoon I meet Hewa, a short round-faced chap from Sri Lanka with a shy ready smile, he is wearing a white safari style short-sleeved uniform with the hospital logo covering the top pocket. Hewa cleans the house once a week. He beams his pleasure at meeting Madame and 'baby'. Tim is horrified to hear himself described this way and draws himself up to his full height of three feet.

'I'm nearly seven.' he informs the hapless Hewa, who, unperturbed says,

"Baby is big, for six!" and sets about ironing our clothes. He seems a bit put out to discover I have already cleaned the house but is quickly reassured that there is a lot still to do. I fall asleep in one of the three bedrooms so don't hear him leave.

Later Col says he is going into town to fill up his diving bottles. The dive shop is in the centre of town called somewhat inappropriately, 'Diebendz'. Colin has been diving for years and the Gulf has many interesting fish and other sea life. His photographs have won him many a competition and a few holidays in prize money.

The loud cry of the muezzin puts paid to any further transactions as we have to sit outside on the pavement with all the other *'infidels'* in the 40° C (104°F) heat—and this at night! A couple of men can't resist his golden hair and they pat Tim on the head in passing. I've heard the local Saudi's are very fond of children (sautéed not fried—only kidding!). At end of short prayer we return to the shops to buy a videocassette recorder. It doesn't take long to find one and a microwave oven. We buy a power surge protector and get a mixer thrown in for free. A quick dash across the busy road to a nearby supermarket finds us chucking in some things into the trolley when prayer time comes round again. Everyone in the supermarket suddenly disappears and the lights go out. Col whispers,

"They've gone to pray. Let's just wait inside."

We push our trolley to a corner of the store and discover a Filipino lurking behind a take away counter. Col asks him if they're open for business and he nods. An order is placed, in whispers, for fried rice, turkey, chicken and tea. It feels somewhat strange to be sitting in an empty shop with the lights off eating turkey and sipping hot tea from a Styrofoam cup. After forty minutes of '*Maghrib*'—Long Prayer, lights go on again, people are let in from outside and we leave our empty plates to resume our shopping with everyone else.

We get a 10% discount for spending five hundred riyals and a free glass with some marmalade. Tim is given a Lion King pencil at the photography shop. All in all, we've done pretty well, tired but reasonably happy with the days events.

I'm shown the compound swimming pool this morning. This is for Westerners only. It is located close to the Filipino residence. The pool is large and the water very warm. They have sections of artificial grass near the pool which look and feel like a spongy green cloth when walked on. I soon discover the Saudi's are fond of the artificial in nature. Fake palms, trails of bright plastic flowers, faux wood and two-metre lurid green 'bushes' dot the city centre. Tim is coaxed into the water by Col. He's apprehensive at first but is soon splashing around in a large orange tyre. I watch them from the side in a lopsided deckchair. A white-cheeked barbet jumps around in a small bush near the wall. I'm suddenly struck that it is the first bird I've seen in three days.

As we leave I'm introduced to a colleague of Col's and his wife who were eating inside the poolside lounge. Naturally should I bump into the wife again I'll most likely just look right through her. She is draped from head to toe in black. She also sports a pair of glasses that perch somewhere in the vicinity of her nose, over the thin cloth of her veil. They give Tim an ice-lolly and offer Col and I a pie each. I remember, just in time, to receive it with my right hand.

"*Shukran!.*" I'm feeling pleased to have remembered the word for thank you.

I sense a smile but it's hard to tell for sure.

Today is Thursday, the Saudi equivalent of the weekend, so we have a bit of a lie-in, till 7:30! Col is going diving again so after a quick breakfast we gather all our things together and drive to the British Club, which is situated at Low Tide bay.

I've taken some of my music tapes to play in the car. It drowns out a few of the 'beep-beep' sounds that occur if we go faster than 120km an hour. This feature is built into all motor vehicles in Saudi in an attempt to remind drivers to slow down. All that actually happens is that people turn their music up, as we do, and drive as fast as they want.

The BA club, a bare stretch of buff coloured sand off the warm still waters of the Gulf Sea, is about twenty minutes from our compound. Shade cloth covers a small area for the divers. A few plastic chairs are hunched around a sunken table as though in conference. A large cement bath lies to one side for rinsing the diving gear. A long prefab building with a tin roof houses the club gear. Across the way from this is another smaller building that serves as the club restaurant. Outside the café a few more tables and chairs are arranged in small clusters. A set of rusty swings and a see saw completes the club amenities.

I am introduced to Cols' diving buddy, Tom, who works as a technician at the pathology lab. He is in his middle fifties, gray haired and affable. Tom's on a single contract here, as are most of the Foreigners. He tells me that many of the wives who have been out to visit their husbands refuse to live in Saudi.

"They just can't adjust to the heat or the way of life," he explains leaning forward to take his diving bottle out of the back of his land cruiser.

"They call it the magic kingdom."

An air valve hisses noisily into the still hot air. Tom closes it and looks up with a smile,

"You'll soon find out why!"

I return a weak smile and wonder what on earth I'm doing here. It is so hot that I make frequent trips into the restaurant to cool down. This building is air-conditioned which makes it all the more pleasant. A cheerful Brit behind the counter serves me.

"Hullo luv, what can I getcha?"

It's hot so I order tea (mad dogs and all that) and have a look around the small room. A number of people are wearing bathing costumes and I'm relieved to learn that the *abaya* can be removed once through the security gate without fear of retribution. It is now 42° C and the sweat is pouring off me in rivulets. I take my tea outside on a small tray (self service here) and sit under a small thatched palm tree with an umbrella table.

Colin and Tom change out of their dive suits and we have lunch outside on the terrace. Tom is from North Yorkshire and he keeps us entertained with stories of his experiences in Saudi. He's been here eight years so he can tell us a thing or two. He says he'd been to Bahrain for a long weekend recently and came back with a side of bacon wrapped in white paper, labeled Veal. That, along with several pork pies, a pile of books and some Turkish delight that he'd bought for the Filipina assistants back at the lab. Firstly he'd got some flak from Customs about the number of books he had bought and was asked what he did with them.

"I read them," he'd responded somewhat truthfully. It must be said there is little to read in Saudi, that is written in English. In any event, they were confiscated on some pretext or other. The Turkish delight also aroused suspicion. He'd remembered to colour in the picture of a naked Aphrodite with a felt tip pen that was decorating the lids. He had not imagined they wouldn't know what Turkish delight was anyway.

"Take it and show us what you will do with it," ordered one of the customs officers suspiciously. Tom obligingly removed one pale pink square, popped it in his mouth and chewed.

"You eat it," he explained somewhat unnecessarily. He was waved through, his packet of bacon and pork pies undetected.

The atmosphere at the club beach is quite nice. The Brits are cheerful and friendly and they joke around a lot. I actually relax for the first time since arriving, entertained by Tom's stories and the gentle lapping of the sea.

The stamp comes down on my inner arm leaving a faint purplish outline of two palm trees. We've just stepped inside what looks like an average club anywhere in the world, except that it sells homemade beer. It is in fact right in the middle of a strict Moslem country. The beer on offer is *Golden,* or *Honeydew*. The choice is simple. Who can resist a beer called 'honeydew?' We place our order and find our way to the humid pool outside.

The *Sandstorms* are playing tonight. Rock n roll punctuates the still hot atmosphere with sweating gyrating bodies and shrieks of mirth. Elbows raise glasses and stories do the rounds about life in Saudi. The case of the recently murdered nurse comes up. Apparently Tom knew someone who had dated Lucy, one of the accused, when he worked there. In any event he seems reluctant to discuss the murder. At the time it was said that nurse Lucy MacLauchlan was convicted of being an accessory to the murder of her Australian colleague Yvonne Gilford. Deborah Parry, her co-accused, was convicted of murder. Yvonne, aged 55, was found in her room earlier in December beaten, stabbed and suffocated to death, at the King Fahd Military Medical Complex in Dhahran.

Lucy and Deborah, had initially admitted to killing Yvonne but later they withdrew their confessions, after claiming they were sexually assaulted by Saudi police. Both were charged with murder and, according to Saudi sources, were convicted after a trial in Dammam.

Saudi law states that Yvonne's family can insist she is publically beheaded. Deborah was to be beheaded after being convicted of the murder and Yvonne was sentenced to eight years in prison and 500 lashes as an accessory. Later King Fahd, had the two women pardoned as a goodwill gesture and they were freed after 17 months in jail. They both insist they were tortured into falsely confessing to the crime.

"Lucy didn't do it." was all Tom would say.

Mrs. Harvey, dressed in a long dark skirt and cardigan—in a temperature of 39°C—meets us just inside the British International school of Al-Khyber. She will be assessing Tim for possible entry to the school. We leave him sitting a little apprehensively at his midget-sized table. Col drives back to work. The taxi driver arrives at the gate five minutes later to collect me.

"To the gold souq please."

I feel very grand saying that. We sit in silence 'till I'm dropped off somewhere near a row of shopping centres. The one I enter, called the Alhabba Souq, is a typically modern building in design, much like all the shopping centres around the world—shiny tiled floors and brightly lit shop windows on different levels with a long elevator in the centre. The difference lies in the rows of covered women sitting in chattering groups like animated garbage bags. Some have cell phones glued to the vicinity of their ears, small silver squares of modern technology outlined against ancient tradition.

I saunter into Al-Jarir one of a chain of stationery shops and come out with some postcards and a book on how to speak Arabic. Figure it can only help. Also buy some cinnamon buns at a small kiosk for the equivalent of a week's wages back home. Everything seems very expensive if I calculate the cost in Rands, so I decide not to and things go a lot smoother after that.

Colin & Tim are swimming at the local pool, leaving me fiddling with the new satellite TV. Suddenly we have a choice, cartoons, history, movies etc. I run to tell the boys, such is the lack of entertainment here, that this is big news! There are no movie houses, no clubs, bars or casinos in Saudi. En route I meet Ranjit, the pleasant Sri Lankan that Col uses to wash his car. He doesn't actually use him to wash his car; he has him do it for him but he's such an accommodating fellow nothing is impossible. Ranjit is always smiling even though there can't be much to smile about. Times are hard for the locals and the pay is often poor.

Later we leave for the airport to fetch Dan McCorrmick, a friend of Cols who moved from Al-Khyber and is living in Jeddah now. Dan's plane arrives more or less on time and before long he strides through the small arrivals gate, smiling as he spots us. I'm suddenly reminded of Tin Tin—the same face and hair! I catch myself looking behind him for Snowy. We have driven to the airport in Dan's yellow box-like Toyota, a huge vehicle with shower facilities in the back. I can't think why anyone would ever want to shower in these cramped confines. Dan drives to another compound where the dive club is situated. The Filipino guard at the gate won't let us in until one of the club members comes out and says we're 'okay'! I blame the car! The dive club consists of two large open rooms with a bar across one end and a large screen against the other wall. Strobe lights swing slowly in the air-conditioned breeze. Col buys me a frothy. It's my third so far and I've only been in Saudi a week. And I was worried I would not see an alcoholic drink till I returned home! I meet some of the members of the club most of whom are British.

Sandy Calger's wife, Macy, isn't British though —she's a plumpish Filipina woman with dark hair and a ready smile. She joins me, and the chairman's wife, June Frightfully-Snobbe. June is telling me she only buys her clothes from Italy and her shoes in London. Turning gratefully to Macy I ask her how she and Sandy had met.

"Oh I was doing *hees* housework *por* him," she says without embarrassment. June's hooded eyes drop a fraction. Her red rouged smile becomes fixed,

"Oh really!" her mouth turns down disapprovingly. A fleeting smile reveals lipstick-stained teeth. Waving in the general direction of the door she mutters,

"*Aye* simply must say hello to my dear friend Doris Horne-Smythe," as she strides off, leaving only the smell of her expensive perfume. I shrug and ask Macy if she has any children. She nods and points over to her two boys who are playing with Tim. No snobbery there, thank heavens.

We chat to various people, sip on home made beer and a short while later Dan drives us back to the hospital in his air-conditioned mobile shower. I'm sitting in the back looking at some of his dive slides through a hand viewer. The water is always flat at the Gulf!

The fax spews some information regarding local schools onto the floor this morning, and I promise myself to phone them later. The British Aeronautical compound also happens to own the local dive club in Half Tide Bay, so we take a drive out there to take a look. There is a small *brown* patch of dusty ground near the entrance proclaiming to be the *golfing green*. A light breeze, albeit a warm one, blows over the desiccated landscape, but it does help to cool things a little.

While the lads go off for a dive I enter the clubhouse for some cokes. The chatty bloke at the restaurant counter tells me it has been quiet this past week as most people are away for the long summer holidays. I speak to a Welsh chap whose wife has just returned home to Wales with their two sons. He says a lot of *ex pats* are leaving now as restrictions are becoming prohibitive due to *Saudi-ization.* He says that ever more strict Islamic laws are being enforced by the religious police, (Muttawan) with renewed vigour these days. He reckons that restrictions on certain perks could mean more people will leave. He has been here four years and the £/Riyal exchange isn't as good as it used to be. I listen to all this with some dismay. Sods law we arrive just as the party is ending, I think somewhat ruefully. Well, nothing for it but to make the best of things.

Tim finds a young British boy to play with and they set about building sand castles and the like, which keeps him happily occupied. The others return from their dive having seen some interesting shrimps, some of which apparently tried to mate with the Perspex lens of Col's underwater camera! Tim and I stroll along the beach and find a spiny fish, a loo roll and a football for our efforts.

The police stop us on the way home—I have just enough time to fling my *abaya* over my exposed shoulders as they scrutinize our visas and agamas for expiry dates, then our marriage certificate for legality, before waving us on.

It's 4:30am and we're up and about to prepare for a boat ride. After a hurried breakfast we collect Tom and set off for Jubail, another coastal area about 45 Km. away to the North of Al Khyber. We pass a typical Bedouin campsite with a small herd of camels wandering outside the tents.

Tom and I are discussing the local newspapers here. I tell him I've noticed how flowery their language is and how the locals love to give long wordy descriptions. Saudi, for example, is the 'most beauteous and wondrous' etc. Tom reckons the best paper to read is the Arab News, aka *The Green Truth,* so called as it is printed on pale green paper. He says it contains a letters page where a *Muttawa* answers questions and gives out advice to general queries about Islam and lifestyles.

(Example: 'my brothers wife is all alone in the world since my brother died; can I make her my wife and keep her company? My other wife would have a friend')

Tom tells us that the Filipinos have a much harder time here than others. At one local hospital Filipina nurses are kept locked behind a barbed wire fence three metres high. They are required to wear name badges with micro chips embedded, linked to a main computer so that all their movements can be monitored. Important stuff, like how long they might spend in the loo or at lunch is carefully recorded. The Filipina are not allowed to receive phone calls and are cut off after ten seconds, should some poor unfortunate person try a real conversation! Ironically though, they are allowed two hours alone in the large shopping centres where Saudi teens apparently meet up with young locals who want some contact with the females. This tête-à-tête is achieved via the omnipresent cell phone. Numbers are scribbled on cigarette boxes and dropped near a veiled individual with an interesting silhouette and pretty eyes! Strange place. Tom calls it the land of lost logic and I'm beginning to see why!

Many small wooden dhows bob up and down on the smooth water of the gulf as we approach the fishing village of Jubail. It looks like an ancient scene, with the ornately carved boughs of their wooden fishing boats and local fishermen. The Gulf fishermen wear distinctive linen skirts. They fling their nets aboard and clamber around the wooden decks of their boats with practiced ease. There is a small group of divers from the club waiting to board. They pass their diving gear aboard with the help of some local sailors. Eventually all the diving bottles (cylinders) are ready in their holders and we are about ready to cast off.

It is stinking hot and only a little shade on board. Colin hands his underwater camera to another diver on the dhow and prepares to follow when suddenly one of the coast guards—who is checking the list of people aboard against their agamas—spots the diving camera. He yells out in Arabic that it is not allowed.

Furthermore, Col's diving knife is also not allowed. He looks around helplessly as another diver has difficulty with his flashgun, insisting that it doesn't take pictures. They don't believe him,

"*mafee cameera*!" they repeat, "No camera!" The two guards are adamant, none of the items mentioned are allowed on board.

Photography is strictly prohibited along the Gulf coast they say (though not in so many words) and the more everyone tries to explain that all the equipment is for diving only the more they insist the stuff remains behind. Col then informs the group that he isn't going to dive and asks them to chuck all his gear off the boat. Tom says the same thing. It costs the equivalent of 30 dollars for a dive on the boat. And obviously it isn't worth that amount if they can't take their gear along. The dhow owner, whom the club had chartered the boat from, meets this news with some dismay. In any event the stuff is offloaded and we decide to spend the day in Jubail at a place called *Pearl beach* located near the Old Town of Al Jubail. It was originally a small fishing village up until 1975 when the new industrial area sprung up.

Some Italians own this expat beach compound. It is pricy to get into but well worth it. A pretty white-sanded beach decorated with tables, deck chairs and palm fronded umbrellas along the still blue sea. A cool air-conditioned restaurant adjoins a shaded verandah. While the guys pull on their gear and wade off into the somewhat shallow water for a dive, Tim and I take a short walk along the beach. The beach itself is full of western foreigners, Italian males to be precise. They lie on their backs in the water, in groups of two or three, chatting in desultory fashion while waves lap gently over hairy pasta-swollen abdomens.

The boys return from the water around 2 o'clock and we all go inside the restaurant for some lunch. The room is decorated with all things nautical. There are shells and driftwood and a small alcove is filled with clay pots. A large boat shaped clock whose hands whizz past the hour in only five minutes hangs on the wall. We order chicken nuggets shaped like animals (we didn't actually ask them to be animal shaped, they just came that way) and a Greek salad. The lads go off for another dive after a suitable period of digestion has passed and Tim submerges like a mushroom in his hat. It becomes so hot I have to wade into the water in my dress, and change into my colourful cotton wrap afterwards. I have to be careful because every time I lift an arm, a boob falls out, affording the floating Italians an eyeful.

The author looking bemused

Chapter Three

"One's destination is never a place, but a new way of seeing things."

Henry Miller

The Hospital

"Where you go?"

The armed security guard leans against the window. He strokes his rifle softly with fat sausage-like fingers and narrows his eyes.

"My wife is going to start work here," offers Col hopefully.

"Where your *iqgama* and gate pass?"

Col extracts his *aqgama* and hands it through the open window,

"Uh, we don't have a gate pass yet. She starts today," nodding towards me.

He glances at the *aqgama* and hands it back,

"Where her aqgama?"

"She not have one," Continues Col patiently in his best Pidgin English, "She work today first one time. Getting tomorrow *aqama* In'sAllah"

"OK go!" He probably hadn't a clue what Col just said.

Colin drives me to the hospital's second gate and deposits me with my sponsor, Al-Ghandi, who demands to see my contract. It appears I'm the only *westerner* for orientation today and there's a pile of papers to complete. The information contains such snippets, such as; *Females are not allowed to wear make-up, jewelry and NO perfume or other smells*! Lest you entice some poor defenseless male, you understand!

A Filipina pathology technician called Irene chats to me. She has apparently worked at the hospital previously but had been granted leave to get married and was now back to 'get pregnant!' Noticing my raised eyebrow, she hastily explains that her husband is also working at the hospital and she has joined him to work here (and presumably 'get pregnant.') She is a pleasant and chatty girl with round cheeks and straight black hair cut in a smooth bob. She helps put me at ease. Dennis is the orientation officer; a rather effeminate Filipino with a shock of Elvis styled gelled hair. He takes us outside into a long narrow room filled with sewing activities to have our uniforms measured.

I'm presented with a long black skirt made of stiff canvas, the consistency and thickness of a tent, and a white puff-sleeved, high-necked blouse over which a long maroon jacket is worn. I look aghast at this Victorian horror and try not to imagine how uncomfortable it's going be in the intense heat!

We meet numerous Arab officials during the course of the day, all with impressively long titles, 'The deputy Director of Al Hammad-Rasool Airbase, Mohamed Al-Hassaini,' and so forth. They are all either sipping mint tea, chatting in small groups, on the phone or just sitting and smoking. None appear to be remotely overworked.

Lastly I am led to my new office in the department of Education and introduced to the secretary, a tall handsome semi-bald Egyptian called Rehaad. Dennis takes his leave with a limp handshake and I'm left with the Egyptian. I notice he has a small calloused spot the size of a dime in the middle of his forehead. Later I learn this peculiar mark serves to illustrate how devout he is (during prayer at the mosque, the continuous motion of the forehead touching the floor in supplication creates the sought after callous.) Rehaad smiles kindly and hands me a copy of my job description.

"Come Janette, (pronounced *shjenette,*) I *weel* show you the education department."

We walk along a short corridor to the Audio-Visual (AV) room and I am introduced to Ding, Victor and Astor, three Filipino men in charge of the hospital audio-visuals. Rehaad tells me sotto voice that they are all lazy good for nothings, but possibly helpful? Ding is small with a mischievous smile and laughing eyes. Astor is a round faced, almost Buddah-like version of Mao Tse Tung and Victor looks like the evil character 'Jafar,' in Aladdin, only with more hair.

"Hi," I offer breezily and they greet me in unison.

Rehaad shows me to my dusty office the size of a small cupboard. Two desks and a bookcase complete the furniture. He tells me I may go home now so I phone Colin, who says he can't fetch me till much later. Rehaad, ever helpful, says not to worry. He will help me get a taxi. Another warm smile,

"Don't worry *Shjenette,*" he pats my arm reassuringly, "I *weel* help you."

He phones 'O-La taxi service. They promise a cab in twenty minutes.

"Who is in charge of the department?" I ask while we are waiting.

"Dr. Mahir Al-Hammad is in charge," he replies, "he is away overseas at the moment and will return when you start next week."

"Thank you for your assistance Rehaad."

When the taxi arrives he explains to the driver in rapid Arabic where he is to drive me. A good thing too, as I haven't a clue where our hospital is located! At the gate of King Waheed Hospital I am asked again for my gate pass, which I don't have. I try pleading with the taxi driver, an Indian, to tell the guard that I live here with my husband, Dr. Mostert. Col's recreation card is thrust into the bewildered guard's hand. He glances at it incomprehensively but notes the hospital logo and he lets me in with a curt wave of his hand.

I am up early to get ready for work. Not too happy about my uniform, the heavy stiff thing can easily stand up by itself! I get around wearing the long sleeved blouse by putting on one of my short-sleeved white tops instead. Only the top of my neck is visible and I am hoping this will pass muster. Colin, as usual has to drive me to work. We drive past long stretches of sand dunes and bits of metal wreckage. Silently wrapped up in our thoughts while the incessant *beeb-beeb* of the land cruisers speed warning sounds in the background. I'm dropped off at gate two, this time armed with my temporary gate pass. After showing it to the guard I wander in early. The secretary Rehaad is already there and he takes me to the main building to meet Leanne Wilson, The American director of nursing (DON). I return the SR100 Rehaad lent me for the taxi the other day. Leanne's secretary offers me some tea while I settle down to wait. When I finally meet her, Leanne is a pleasant woman; short brassy blond hair that screams, 'fake,' verified by her ID photo showing her with very dark hair! She has thin lips that are outlined darkly and coloured in with bright red lipstick. Leanne motions me to a seat and begins to explain what she wants from me in her slow American drawl. We seem to understand each other, which is to say I understand the jargon and agree with most of it! However, I'm still a bit confused as to who I actually report to, as Dr. Al-Hammad is my boss in the Education department and she is in charge of nursing. Time will tell because she isn't.

Two medical doctors run the Education department, with Rehaad as secretary, an English teacher and the three AV guys making up the team. I am to be the Nursing Education supervisor. My main task it seems is to teach all the nursing staff new procedures and maintain quality of work performance through in-service training.

Ding, the small mischievous looking Filipino from AV takes me along to the finance department to get an advance on my salary. This is apparently standard practice for newcomers. The Saudi official at the desk looks up briefly from his morning newspaper and coffee and says,

"I can't assist you today, *in's Allah* tomorrow!" before returning to his paper.

We amble along to the security department for my hospital ID and gate pass. Ding stops frequently to chatter to various acquaintances in Tagalog, the language most widely spoken in the Philippines. Again we hear, "maybe next week, *ins'Allah*". "The photo machine is broken". I am starting to hear a lot of the word, *Ins'Allah*, literally meaning, 'If God wills it' and I am very soon to learn that God seldom appears to will it!

We return to the Education dept. where I meet Dr. Mahir Al-Hammad himself, a pleasant looking chap of around thirty-five, dressed in Western style. He is of medium build, olive skinned with short curly black hair and a trim moustache and beard. He welcomes me with a weak handshake. He has a peculiar way of speaking without looking directly at one, gazing downwards instead or to one side of your head. I find myself looking over my shoulder a few times until I realize he is actually talking to me. He mutters vaguely that he hopes I will be happy and he is sure everyone will be able to help me to settle down. He ushers me into his small office. He has a large wooden desk with three telephones and his computer, standing on one side, is covered with a small blue prayer mat.

We discuss long and short-term goals which all lean towards having a strong routine and good administration. Suddenly he reaches down into his small fridge, which stands alongside his desk and he extracts a tissue-wrapped can of mango juice from within. Clasping the cold can in one hand; I gaze earnestly at him and declare my strong belief in structure as I pull the tab. Before taking a sip, I mention that I *love* writing reports. He looks relieved. Says he will organize Col's gate pass so that he may enter the outer gate and drop me off closer to the office. It will save me about a kilometer's walk. He then leads me back to my office and waves vaguely in the direction of the file covered bookcase, suggesting I read through my predecessors notes to get an idea of things. I sit at my desk as he closes the door, trying to assimilate the morning's activities so far. I start reading through some notes and make some of my own. The first starts with the sentence: 'I haven't a clue where to start!'

Ding brings me a Coke-lite and asks for the ring pull. Apparently if you get seventy-five of these you can win a watch! He's a sweet chap and I gladly hand over the ring pull. It's the least I can do. He's off with a grin. Midday prayers announce themselves suddenly via a set of loudspeakers in the office and I am startled out of my concentration with the sudden wailing. *'Allah, Allah Akbar. Mohammed Rasool.'*

Aster pops his head around the door and says I can go to the, "*Capeteeria* p*or yor lunch.*" Later Ding shows me a typewriter that I may use if I need to make notes. He says I can use it in their office as it would be, "more *comportable por* you." The Filipino cannot say the letter 'f' easily. It is quite amusing to hear them talk, especially when the sentence contains multiple 'fs'!

I see Leanne again this morning to discuss what she'd like me to do with the nurses in terms of training. I leave her office an hour and a half later not much the wiser but with a whole lot of gossip under my belt.

Back at the department, Rehaad introduces me to his pregnant wife who is visiting him from the clinic where she works. It turns out we have already met on my first day in the Path lab. I am embarrassed to remember having given her unsolicited advice about her pregnancy. I discover she works in the primary health care clinic and could probably tell me a thing or two. She is veiled when first we are introduced but a while later she unveils herself to chat a bit. She is an attractive woman, pale olive complexion, almond eyes and a voluptuous mouth. Rehaad is pleased when I tell him so.

A short while later I am struggling to put one of my gold hoop earrings in my ear, so I go back to Rehaad's office to ask for his wife's help. Rehaad informs me she has left a few minutes earlier but insists on helping me himself. A few minutes later he performs this strangely intimate gesture in this heavily Islamic environment. I feel uncomfortable as he gently inserts the gold hoops through my reddening lobes and I rush off as soon as the earrings are in place.

Ding offers to take my photo negatives into town for processing. The Filipino are a wealth of information and it is advisable to get to know them if you need to get the best advice or assistance in finding anything out in Saudi.

After eating my take-away chicken and rice alone in my office (still too shy to sit by myself in the cafeteria) Dr. Al-Hammad collects me and he walks with me to the security office—after a quick prayer in his office—to sort out the problem of Col's gate pass. It is done within the hour. I thank him profusely; apparently Allah was willing this time. It will make a great difference in getting through the gates every morning. Naturally he has his own reasons for getting me to work on time!

I go with Rehaad on a walkabout. He seems to know everyone here and is especially fond of chatting up the women. He is busy charming the *abaya* off this veiled woman in the library, who he later informs me is at least sixty years old and as ugly as a witch! No luck with getting an advance on my pay yet. We meet the chief finance officer outside on our way back to the Education dept. I am introduced and my plight made known to him. The officer, dressed in the national white *thobe* and headgear says he will follow it up. It will be ready soon, '*ins'Allah.*' It was this last assertion that should have alerted me but I am new to the game and my Arabic vocabulary is limited.

At around 4:10 the AV lads appear at my door and announce that it is time to leave and we must lock up. As Colin does not yet have his gate pass I am forced to clock out earlier than normal and walk the very hot kilometer walk to gate number One. Colin arrives with Tim to find me hot and bothered sweating in my Victorian garb and not very pleased with life in general.

As mentioned, although Thursday is generally considered the start of the weekend, but I still have to work till lunchtime. It is so hot and humid that my sunglasses steam up and I can see nothing out of them. My office is locked when I get there so I walk to the auditorium where I find Victor and Ding setting up for a medical lecture. A large silver urn, some Styrofoam cups, teabags and coffee powder are available on a trolley for anyone attending the lecture (plus a few who don't!) I sip my tea and wait to see what happens next. The daily routine is still new to me. Slowly the auditorium begins filling up, mostly with doctors and radiologists, who shuffle up to pour themselves some hot tea or coffee before making their way inside. The lecture is to start punctually at nine, but at half past there is still no sign of the speaker or even a halfway decent crowd inside.

Fifteen minutes later an Egyptian doctor with sparse hair and thick dark glasses takes to the podium. Without preamble he begins a talk on *fractured penises*. I am momentarily taken aback but no one seems to think this is a strange topic for a Thursday (read Saturday) morning lecture. In fact, most of the audience appears to be dozing off as the doctor continues in a halting, laboured drone. He shows a few slides to illustrate a point (no pun intended) and at 10:30 the lecture finishes, as abruptly as it began.

It is still very hot outside and sweat pours off my face and into my high-necked blouse. The skirt is so stiff that it could walk without me and the unbecoming maroon jacket increases the sauna effect to the maximum. I bump into a blonde haired girl wearing the same outfit as I in the foyer. She stops and introduces herself as Delia Hardcastle, a Canadian who works as a medical transcriptionist. We chat a while and she tells me where I can buy a three dimensional map of Al-Khyber, which will help with getting around. Delia invites me to her office for coffee or a 'soda pop' whenever I'm in need and then dashes off to a meeting. What a nice friendly woman, I'm thinking as I head back towards the Education Department.

Back at the office I decide to visit the *comfort* room. This is the one and only toilet in the Education building. I share it with the seven other males who work here and I hate it on sight! The floor and toilet seat are wet for reasons which I only discover later, (sensitive readers look away) have more to do with cleaning of feet before prayer than cleaning of nether regions, which they do with vigour using the nozzle water spray that accompanies each Eastern style loo! I have heard that the Filipinos, with whom I have to share the toilet, actually stand on the seat while urinating! Judging from the state of the floor, they must wash their hands with the bidet nozzle! Later I ask them to try and keep the 'comport' room clean, as I have to use it as well. They all nod but it stays the same for the remainder of my stay. I soon become used to hovering a few centimeters above the toilet in an attempt to avoid sitting on a damp seat! My thighs ache terribly the first few times I have to levitate but I soon build up admirable quadriceps muscle tone and it's not long before I am able to hover for at least five minutes without contact.

Col returns from his night dive in good spirits. He has seen some very colourful reef fish after a few dives. I leave him hauling the dive equipment into one of our baths to soak. Tim and I try to visit the gym but it isn't easy to get in. There is an irritating male/female hour rule and booking in advance is essential (even though the place has been empty the four times I've been). The recreation card has to be produced before being allowed to use the equipment. Women's hour is naturally the inconvenient time of 10H00, which is when I am at work. The male times coincide with most evening prayer times as well so I'm not sure how many people actually benefit!

"Why does the recreational building not open at a more convenient time, like 6pm?" I ask the Supervisor. He picks his teeth and says Colin, as my husband, has to complain. Why am I not surprised?

In any event when Tim and I actually get it right a few days later, we are surprised and a little disappointed—given the red tape to get there—that it is largely just an empty room. A huge mirror runs the length of one wall. Two broken exercise bicycles and an odd assortment of weights complete the equipment. We wander around some more and discover a room with table tennis.

There are the usual difficulties to find anyone to unlock cupboards, extract keys, and sign books for the paddles and ball, just to have a quick game. Tim's game plan seems to involve trying to keep the ball *off* the table, so I manage to get some exercise after all, just by leaping around!

I find an abandoned pair of Arabian women's shoes lying in a flowerbed. They are pointy toed and have gold buckles and hearts all over them. I decide to take them home with me as an interesting talking point. The heads of small children peer at us through the windows, we smile and wave and they drop back giggling. We get back at 7pm, tired and somewhat pensive. We are both still adjusting to this strange new world we find ourselves in.

Chapter Four

*"Travel is more than the seeing of sights;
it is a change that goes on, deep and
permanent, in the ideas of living."*

Miriam Beard

Gold plated bidet

THIS AFTERNOON WE leave for Half Tide beach after lunch so Col can get a dive. As we drive through the gates, he tells me he's forgotten his goggles so he can't dive after all. He's grumpy and Tim starts to perform as well. I feel like telling the pair of them that it's my day off too!

We decide to have a short drive along the beach. The land cruiser handles the small dunes very well, even in normal drive. We stop and get out for a closer look at the sea, which is a beautiful aquamarine colour. The beach however is not that beautiful. It's covered in all kinds of rubbish, left over items, litter and sea debris. I stroll around the sea edge while Tim paddles nearby. After some minutes I have collected some shells, a glass, a T-shirt, a rusty knife and a garden chair in perfect state of repair! I spy a huge Persian carpet half buried in the sand, in good condition except for a slight tear at one corner. I want to drag it back with me but Col refuses to let me to take it. Spoilsport! I decide to wade into the sea with Tim and have a little fun with him. I am laughing and lifting my skirt against the gentle waves when I hear Col calling. I look up and see one of the Coast Guard vehicles has pulled up along side ours. One of the guards is speaking with Col who looks worried. I run up to them and ask what's up.

"Where your marriage certificate"? Asks one of the guards without preamble, looking from me to Col as though to determine from our faces whether or not we are actually married. While I'm searching through my bag for the certificate, Tim rushes out of the sea and comes up to see what is going on. The guards look from Tim to Col and back to me and decide we must be legitimate. He waves his hand to indicate that I can stop looking and with no further conversation they climb back into their car and drive away.

Apparently these guys don't guard people's lives so much as guard the coast from people! They seem to spend most of their time preventing people from having or seeming to be having any fun! One gets the idea they'd drive past a drowning person to stop a man and a woman from being seen standing next to each other (known locally as 'ugly mixing').

We later stop to look at a stretch of beach that was donated to our hospital as a gift from a visiting prince. The beach was duly fenced off and padlocked at great cost to the hospital. At the last moment the authorities decide that there might be too much of the aforementioned *mixing* taking place should the proposed opening go ahead. The beach now stands empty, encircled by an expensive wire fence. Col is sure he's missing out on a good diving spot! Though why all the good diving should be had at the exact place we have no access to, I can't say. An outline of wild camels on the horizon stirs some excitement; Camelus dromedaries, the one humped variety are my first in Arabia. I take a few snaps with my small digital camera.

I have a surreal chat with Dr. Al-Hammad this morning. He invites me into his small office, asks me to sit then asks me how I am, how I am settling in and continues with the assertion that he's sure Darlene's information is helping me. Not wanting to give him the idea that I have no idea who Darlene is, seeing as he appears to hold her in high esteem, I reply that she has been very helpful. He explains the importance of maintaining the high standard of education in his department regardless of what "they" may think. I nod uncertainly, not wanting to ask who 'they' may be, then dash off after this short exchange to find Rehaad, and ask him who the heck Darlene is and where can I find her. Rehaad smiles and shakes his balding head,

"Darlene, she is the educator before you. She left a year ago," he informs me. Apparently she is a well-liked Canadian who left for a better paying position at Saudi Aramco in the East.

"How can I contact her?"

He tells me about ARAMCO, the huge American oil based company that is co-owned by the USA and Saudi.

"She is staying there since last November," he informs me. "I *weel* give you the number of the hospital."

I return to my small office, sit behind my desk and stare at the overflowing files that protrude from the bookcase set against one wall. It all looks such a mess. I feel anxious. Darlene would know what to do. I am sure she wouldn't have to stare at the walls trying to think of something to occupy her time.

Everyone seems to be expecting me to start work but I haven't even had the benefit of orientation or induction yet. The education department continues to be depressing as I attempt to make sense of everything. No one assists or explains anything. As a result I spend most of the day sitting at my desk trying to work out what to do and how to go about teaching the staff. Apart from the head nurses who are all from UK, America, Ireland or South Africa, the majority of the Registered nurses are Filipino with some South African or Sri Lankan's.

I have many years experience in teaching student nurses of all levels but here they are all postgraduates, so to speak. I don't yet know their level of training or what their needs are. Perhaps that's where I must start, I think decisively and gather up my papers.

Rehaad comes in and asks for a photograph of me with Aster, Ding and Victor. I stand in the middle of the room surrounded by small Filipino's and smile into the camera. I'm amused at his sense of priority.

Passing another small office en route to mine, I peer in and see Mohammed, a stern looking man in army fatigues behind his desk. He wears a thick untidy beard and gold-rimmed glasses. I later note that he dons the army uniform during normal working hours, the rest of the time he wears the *thobe* and *iqal*. His position in the company is *Muttawa*.

A Saudi flag lies limply on one side of his table and he's writing something on a piece of lined paper. As he looks up, I realize with a jolt, that this is the same man I had earlier asked where the toilet was.

"Good morning." he says and stares at me for a second or two.

I return his greeting a bit sheepishly and flee to the confines of my office.

"Will I ever get it all right"? I think anxiously. In fact I feel suddenly very miserable. I have a quick weep, phone Col at work then decide to walk over to the main building and have some lunch. The menu consists of chicken in an assortment of guises so I opt for a cheese sandwich from one of the vendors.

Word must have got round because I receive a telephone call from one of the nursing supervisors who says she'd like to show me around the hospital and introduce me to various key people. Doreen, as I am asked to call her, is an American, judging from her accent and she wears the white nurse's uniform, which is buttoned up to her neck. She has a white turban and veil, which effectively covers her hair. She must be married to a Saudi, I think, until she makes some disparaging remark about them so decide then that her husband is probably Egyptian. She is softly spoken and I find myself walking at right angles in order to hear her quiet comments as she shows me around the hospital.

There are wide gleaming corridors between admin and the wards. Huge portraits of the three sovereigns—King Said, Prince Abdullah and Prince Sultan—watch over the staff as they scurry to and fro up the wide staircase leading to the upper wards. I am introduced to the heads of department as we walk around. I notice that a uniformed guard sits at the entrance to all the female wards. His job, Doreen whispers to me as we pass, is to ensure no unauthorized male enters the female ward.

The wards are clean and bright with matching accessories, a far cry from the government hospitals back home. Doreen takes me to the 'number one' VIP suite.

"This is for the king," she informs me, turning the big brass doorknob. We enter a room of such opulence and luxury; it might be situated in a top five-star hotel instead of a hospital. A bowl of red grapes adorns a huge mahogany table to one side of the front room. The suite consists of an outer waiting room furnished with huge sofa's and chairs in red and gold brocade, long velvet curtains with gold tasseled tie-backs and an inner waiting room with leather desks, red Persian carpets, a huge drinks cabinet. I briefly wonder whether it might also contain some alcoholic beverage.

"We make sure there's enough whisky for the king when he comes here," Doreen says reading my mind. I raise my eyebrow but she just shrugs and says, 'They get used to drinking stuff like that when travelling abroad.' Doreen leads me to a hospital bed with all manner of technology to ensure His Majesty's every comfort. A huge TV screen sits in front of the bed. The bathroom is unbelievable. Everything is gold plated; the taps, the toilet handle, even the bidet plug and toilet brush is made from twenty-four carat gold!

"Imagine peeing onto a gold plated plug," I chuckle. Doreen ignores my comment.

"The first thing they do when arriving is order ten phones," she says closing the door behind her and locking it carefully. "For some reason they seem to think they need more than one."

"Another problem we have here," she continues, "is that many of the patients don't leave." I look astonished.

Who would want to stay indefinitely in a hospital?

"Many of the Saudi women come in for a rest. Whether they give birth, have check ups or need specific treatment, they all stay long after they are discharged."

The reason, she explains, is that the Saudi men are very demanding with regards their conjugal rights. These poor women find the only way they can take a break from unwanted spousal attention is to stay for long periods in hospital. They tend to provide the wrong home telephone number and address so that any attempt to have them discharged is thwarted. They will leave only when they have had a good rest and hospital becomes boring. It's not only the females who linger however. There is apparently one male who has been in the hospital since 1995! Generally the ward turnover of patients is very slow. I am surprised to note that the ICU is very quiet and has in fact only one patient, despite having eight beds available. I'm betting they don't want to remain too long in *this* department as the cost is usually double the normal rate. Doreen leads us via another long corridor to another unit. I meet Dorette, the head nurse, who is also from South Africa.

"May I introduce you to our new Education manager," says Doreen smiling at some small dark haired nurses dressed in loose blue trousers and lightweight jackets,

"Janette Mostert this is *Purification*, our senior nurse. This is *Glorification* her assistant, and this is *Post Partum.*"

"Pardon?" I exclaim. This last name is too strange, even for a catholic Filipino. Turns out the latter is in reference to the station we're in; part of the Gynae ward. We continue to the next unit on the ground floor.

A notice pasted on the wall in theatre proclaims: *floggings shall continue until morale improves.* Someone has a sense of humour here, I think, in relief.

My tour of the hospital ends at the Infection Control department office, a bright cheerful room with a large picture window overlooking the manicured grounds of the hospital. It has the obligatory line of windblown palm trees. I think of my small, dark, depressing office and momentarily wish I'd applied for a job in infection control.

Ruth, a red haired Canadian, is the infection control nurse. She wears large glasses and a smile to match. She welcomes me with an offer of a *soda pop*. I have a Fanta, and drink it gratefully, while she fills me in on the workings of trying to keep King Waheed Hospital under control from an infection point of view. She says it is an ongoing affair. Doreen takes me back to the education department and asks me when I'm planning the next CPR lecture. "Soon!" I promise closing the door after her.

Today the Muttawa stops me en route to my office and asks my name.

"Uh, I'm Janette, the new educator," I stammer. He hands me a folded piece of paper with his name written in Arabic and in which four succulent dates nestle. I receive them somewhat dubiously, hoping this is the beginning of a beautiful friendship and not some trap for the Western hussy who dared to ask where the toilet was. I'm wearing open toed sandals this morning and my red painted nails wink suggestively up at him. I'm sure I've offended him already but, no, he's smiling at me.

"My name is Mohammed"

I venture a slight grin, thank him for the dates and shuffle off to my office to eat them.

"Maybe not all *Muttawan* are bad news," I think popping the last delicious sweet into my mouth. Later on I manage to get some sort of CPR programme going, in outline anyway. Mel, the South African Head nurse from the clinic takes me to the admission office run by Filipinos to collect my *bataga*, or medical card. Without it I would have to pay for the medical services that are otherwise part of my contract perks. En route she tells me about the staff doctor, who is quite a *Lothario* and apparently examines your chest for everything from sore tonsils to swollen legs.

I have to laugh. As we return to the Education building we hear Astor yelling down the *pone*. He seems to think it's necessary to shout at anyone he phones. I'm tempted to ask him to 'phone Frederick for the fill-in form' just for a crack.

Col tells me this evening (apropos of nothing) that if you fatally hit a camel on the road you have to compensate the owner—not only for the loss of his camel—but for the all potential offspring the animal might have had. Doesn't matter if the camel is a castrated hundred-year-old three legged male with no future prospects whatsoever; you pay dearly for your mistake. So, as in Africa, if you hit anything alive put your foot down and drive like crazy!

It is easily 50° C (122°F) today but the state doesn't ever admit to this. A rule made by the king a few years back states that no-one may work if the temperature is over 50°C, so it never officially goes beyond 49°C! This minor adjustment naturally makes not a whit of difference to the Pakistani workers trying to complete a building on site. Some have died of heat exhaustion.

"The first policy we need to look at," says Hala Al-Katani, who tries and fails to chair the meeting, is 'How to comb the hair of a patient that is very curly.' She frowns, and I sigh in disbelief, "What nonsense!"

We are sitting around a long wooden table listening to Hala list a number of policies that need updating, most of which are archaic and obsolete.

"Pursed lip breathing!" I snort derisively and next thing I know I'm on the review committee together with Sue from *Paeds*, Cathy from Male *Meds* and Debs from *Surg*. (They're big on abbreviations here)!

Back at the office Ding presents me with my official name badge. My name is written in Arabic. It reads:

جانيت موسترت (Janette Mostert) التمريض المربـ (Nursing Educator.) I'm quite pleased with it and attach the badge immediately onto the stiff fabric of my maroon jacket.

The day limps on in slow motion. Later I meet Sue, a short stern gray haired woman with a Geordie accent, and Cathy, large ginger haired lass with at least three earrings in each ear. So much for the dress code policy I think wryly.

They are part of the policy review committee and they tell me we will meet twice a week to work on the long list of policies we had discussed earlier. Me and my big mouth!

I'm in the dental nurse's office facing a row of grinning dentures set in cement. Venturing further into the room a round gray haired woman comes into view, sitting back in a huge easy chair reading what appears to be a novel. A cigarette dangles from her lips. She looks up unperturbed at this intrusion, not at all embarrassed about being caught relaxing during work hours.

"Hello," she says looking over her glasses,

"Who are you"? She has an English accent. I tell her who I am, although the longer I'm here the more debatable it's becoming. She takes a long drag from her cigarette, removes a pen from her top pocket and consults an appointment register.

"You were supposed to be here at 7am."

"Well no-one told me that," I say annoyed.

She tells me not to worry and kindly reshuffles the appointment and after a short while I find myself in a reclining dentist chair with my head practically touching the floor.

While the blood slowly leaves my feet and pools somewhere around my eyes, the Pakistani doctor takes this opportunity to speak and act at the same time.

"Vat is the problem"? He asks shoving several cold, sharp instruments into my open mouth. I gurgle out my complaint using a range of wild eyeball movements for emphasis. From my upside down position his masked mouth hovers above dark eyes over which bushy eyebrows undulate menacingly like hairy caterpillars. He places what must be a small winch into my mouth and stretches it open to its absolute limit. Any wider and he'd be able to see my last meal. He then places several more instruments inside. I try desperately not to swallow when suddenly the phone rings and Doctor Sadist leaves to answer his call. It appears a colleague is phoning in sick.

"You are the second *von* to call in sick," I hear the dentist inform his colleague.

"OK I *vill* cover you up." He nods his head from side to side.

This is not good news, neither for him nor for me as it turns out. He returns to my prostrate head and takes out his frustration for this extra workload by shoving what feels like an entire dishcloth into my already straining mouth. Swallowing by now is totally impossible and I fear suffocation by cloth. My hands wave wildly in the air as he leans over me, stuffing in the last little bit of material, muttering darkly in Urdu. This is a new experience in dentistry. I now have three instruments, two gloved hands and a tablecloth in my mouth. Just as I'm about to claw his eyeballs out, he relinquishes some of the pressure and slowly extracts the cloth, which must have absorbed most of my body fluid. I flail around wildly in the chair trying again to swallow.

"I *vill* finish soon". Says my tormentor,

"Do not try to swallow. Just breathe through your nose."

I have trouble breathing at all, never mind through my nose.

It suddenly dawns on me, as he slowly drills away at my teeth that it is Ramadan. He is Moslem and has not eaten or drunk anything since possibly 3.00 this morning, and the possibility of a mug of coffee at his next break is just not going to happen. I know how I would feel deprived of my tea. The same thought must have occurred to him. He jabs at my gum with his drill and I scream in pain, eyes watering helplessly. Suddenly he begins rapidly removing instruments and without warning I am swung upright and catapulted out of the chair into a standing position. I stagger around trying to regain my balance. The good doctor has meanwhile disappeared under a tap and is now rinsing his entire head with water! I back away hastily thanking him for his time and vouching never to darken his doorstep again. I'd rather pull my own teeth out with a pair of rusty pliers than repeat the experience.

CHAPTER FIVE

"A journey is best measured in friends, rather than miles."

Tim Cahill

Lindy Arrives

I AM STARTLED OUT of my daydream at my desk by Rehaad leading a plump and rather scared looking blond into the office.

"This is Belinda Simons who will be helping you," he says with a nod then leaves us to it.

"Hi, and welcome to the magic kingdom," I say springing out of my chair.

"That's your desk," pointing to the only other desk in the room. I had earlier left a welcome note on her desktop and she sits down and reads it quickly before looking up and smiling.

"Are you from South Africa"?

I reply that although we live there now I was born in UK. She lives in Durban with her husband and three children. She had to leave them all behind in Durban being the only one able to get a job in Saudi. She is obviously still in shock and that is something I can relate to. We chat about our relative experiences in getting to Saudi, and then I quickly fill her in on how things work (or not, as the case may be) in the Education department. I chat non-stop for about forty minutes barely pausing for breath. It is so good to be able to speak to someone who would understand my experiences so far. I eventually pause when I see her dazed expression.

"Well, that's enough for now," I say briskly, getting up from my seat and moving purposefully towards the door. "I'm going to make us a cup of tea and then show you around."

Lindy, as she asks to be called, has been given a room at the Corniche centre. She tells me the hospital bus route took only twenty minutes. I show her around the department, which doesn't take long. I tell her, drinking my tea and pointing in the general direction. "Opposite that is the Audio-Visual guys' office." I will introduce her to them later. *Dr. Who's* office is closed, as it has been ever since I've started. Dr. Who isn't his real name of course but I can't remember his real name and never manage to find out in all the time I'm there. He is the Lebanese doctor who assists Dr. Al-Hammad in the medical wards. He is mainly responsible for teaching the Saudi medical students.

"Dr. Al-Hammad's office is to the right, next to the front door." I continue. There is Rehaad's office, which leads to another office at the end for Mr. Aziz who I also have not yet met. A very small and narrow pantry houses the kettle and some cracked mis-matching cups. There is a small fridge under the counter for the milk and whatever else that needs to be kept cool. The other locked door belongs to the resident Muttawa. The *comfort room* completes the tour of the education building. Lindy gazes in horror at the toilet with three inches of 'water' on the floor. "I will just have to keep it in," she says firmly.

I offer to take Lindy around to introduce her to the head nurses in the various wards. I introduce Sue, Kath, Debs. Shirl and Sunette, another South African who is in charge of Maternity or *post partum* as it is known. Mel heads the maternity clinic. She is the person responsible, in a manner of speaking, for getting me the job in Saudi. An attractive girl, Mel dives in her spare time and Col had asked her to present my CV before we got here.

I introduce Lindy to some of the secretaries and typists such as Delia, the Canadian who has befriended me on my first day and then to big Sue. Our last port of call is the canteen, as we are both feeling peckish by now. I glance at Lindy's generous frame, cased from head to foot in the same thick canvas skirt and long maroon coat as I have, and I feel sorry for her in the excessively hot weather. I'm not to know now that she would transform from an overweight shy and pale-faced woman into a vibrant, slim, tanned blonde, who would soon be having the time of her life!

Lindy is later whisked away by Rehaad to have a blood sample taken. Even though it is a Saudi requirement for all expats to have their blood tests done with their job application for various diseases such as HIV and AIDS, for some reason the process is repeated once they arrive in the country. We later hear that she is off till Saturday when the results of her blood tests will be ready.

Col leaves for Jeddah. He is having a short diving holiday and will return on Saturday. Tim and I are waiting for the *family* bus to arrive. Streams of wilting Filipinos wait patiently in the heat for the *Singles* buses (one for males and one for females!)

After twenty minutes the bus arrives and we board gratefully. Ten minutes later the driver, a Saudi, suddenly pulls over en route to town. The woman next to me whispers that he is going to pray. He disembarks taking with him his *sajjāda* (a small colourful prayer mat), which he unfolds and faces, in the general direction of Mecca. All Muslims need to know which direction Mecca lies from the point at which they are praying from. The mat is to keep the user from getting dirty as well as affording some degree of comfort during *salat* (prayer). Moslems perform *wudu* or ablution of their body before they pray, and the place of prayer needs to be clean, which is not always possible, as in this case.

Tayammum, the Islamic act of dry ablution using sand or dust, takes place when sufficient amounts of water for ritual washing are not available. In this case, sand, earth, stone or clay may be used in its place. When praying, a niche at the top of the mat must be pointing to Mecca. Our driver's prostration takes some twenty minutes and we are forced to wait in the hot bus wilting until he's done. Duty completed, he rolls up his dusty mat, returns to the drivers seat and heads off towards Al-Khyber. Not a word of explanation has passed his lips. I'm glad my companion has explained his actions to me beforehand. We are deposited in a sandy vacant parking lot and walk from there towards the town centre.

I am worried for Tim whose cheeks are turning red in the heat. A woman who has travelled with us kindly advises me where to find a taxi and tells me where we can find the bus back to the hospital. We walk along the dusty side streets of Khyber; streets that are full of rotting vegetables, rusting bits of metal and discarded clothing. We pass humid air conditioners, effluent and Saudi males lying in various poses of inactivity on chairs, along pavement steps and anywhere they can find a spot. An elderly man lies asleep on one such steaming air conditioner.

Tim and I shop in the local bookshop called Al Jarir. It is delightfully cool inside. Although the magazines are few and poor in variety, all have seen the thick black censorious pen of the vice police, and all the women on their pages sport strange black scribbles as clothing which ensure no flesh is shown in support of the poor local males' sensitivities. There's nothing exciting about any of the magazines on offer so we leave and head towards Tammimi, a grocery store selling anything from food to plants.

We have forty-five minutes till the bus from KWH arrives so I ask our taxi driver to recommend a good teashop for me. He takes us to *The broasting Duck,* an unlikely name for tea I think, but well named for its boiling hot conditions. We continue to sweat litres as we step into what turns out to be a fast food joint.

I order a coke and some fish for Tim and I have mint tea. The driver joins us at the Formica table and orders a greasy sausage roll. I feel sure Tim and I should be sitting somewhere else, like upstairs in the family room. This is undoubtedly the single male part of the shop. The large window, however affords us the luxury of viewing passing activity inside as well as out on the street. Huge males wolf down equally large plates of food. One Local throws back his *ghutra* and stares at the large mirror behind the counter. He starts to pick his unsightly teeth. I feel uncomfortable about sitting at the table with our taxi driver, so I hurry Tim along and try to glug down my Styrofoam cup of hot, frothy, overly sweetened tea. I am now that hot and sweaty myself, that I fear I may slide out of my *abaya* altogether. I can't seem to drink my tea fast enough and tell the driver that we should go, as time is running out. To press the point I stand and take my cup with me, determined to finish it in the car. It is virtually impossible to drink boiling hot tea in a car without spilling it. The taxi driver keeps handing me tissues from the front and eventually hands me the whole box. Tim and I giggle as we try to finish our tea and coke without further ruining the taxi's clean interior. We manage to get to the bus in time and stagger aboard laden with packages. I sit down and smile conspiratorially at Tim; we have successfully made our first trip into town by ourselves.

The rest of the weekend passes uneventfully, some would say it lacked excitement and they'd be right. I make two suppers, one to freeze for later (clever girl!) The next few days go by quickly as Lindy and I both adjust to the system, which is at this stage not very clear. We are both exceedingly pleased to have each other for company and we spend many hours talking about what our role is expected to be and how on earth we are to get into some sort of work routine. Lindy was hired specifically to teach the ICU staff as this is where her expertise lies. Lindy tells me about her family and her heartache at having to leave them all behind. Her husband manages a chain supermarket back home. Her three children range from seven to seventeen, her youngest being about Tim's age. Together we while away the hours, left mostly to our own devices. This includes developing a work routine. Cardio-pulmonary-resuscitation (CPR) is one of the first training needs that I see as a matter of urgency, judging from the number of staff shuffling up to the department to ask when the next in-service will be. I have to ensure every staff member has a current CPR record and update those who don't. They call it *recertification*. With not having had a trainer the previous year, this means in effect that everyone needs updating.

I post the dates on the general notice board and pretty soon my first group of medical doctors straggle in for their refresher session, mostly Saudi, Egyptian and

Syrian. The Saudi group is the worst and I fail most of them. They don't appear to know the first thing about saving a life nor do they appear remotely interested. I later realize that this of course relates to their belief that anything that happens is *'in'sAllah'*—the will of God. It is pointless trying to save someone when his or her demise is written, *fait accomplis*. All of this is compounded by the fact that there is no way in hell (or whatever the Islamic equivalent is) that they are going to provide the kiss of life to any woman who is not their own kin! Makes things complicated and rather a challenge.

The Filipina nurses come in their droves, as renewing their contract is dependent on having the updated CPR certificate. This is written in both Arabic and English and the bane of my life becomes signing hundreds of these things every month. Lindy teams up with me on occasion, which helps speed up the process somewhat. And so the first few months pass by with Lindy becoming more and more immersed into the single expat way of life while I try to find my feet as a married woman on a single contract. She very quickly adapts to life in the nurses home.

She has met an Englishman called Len while visiting with a friend in another compound. Len works for the infamous Bin Laden Company in one of their many businesses. The family of the well-known Osama! Len has a wife and two children in the UK. Lindy starts going out with him to play darts at another compound. Saudi's social scene for expats takes place around the compounds. Unlike ours, which by necessity is mostly Saudi—as it forms part of the hospital grounds—these mostly English compounds have an almost normal life, once behind the security gates. Normal means in this case that the dress code is relaxed; people wander around in shorts and T-shirts and it is a close community. It is here where the expats make up the fabric of social life, which is as close to *Western* as they can manage. Their compounds generally have all the amenities such as tennis courts, swimming pools and clubs; a well-stocked library and small grocery shop are all commonly found in the compound grounds. Pakistani males usually run the compound shops.

Debs from *male med* tells me about the Saudi women who come in to give birth. They are usually accompanied by their husbands who stand by pointing to a doll or a crude drawing of the female body hanging behind the door. The doctor has to ask the husband to explain her symptoms to him whilst pointing to any body part using the doll or drawing. Apparently they keep themselves totally covered when they give birth, exposing only their lower body. Some doctors have never actually seen what their female patients look like, having only seen certain parts of their body!

"Och hen, that's nothing," Debs' Scots accent is almost as broad as she is.

"There's many a husband that's *nivver* seen his wife's face. He's more familiar with her nether regions!" She shakes her large frame in silent mirth.

I decide I don't want to walk around in a tent any longer and set about writing a short motivation for both Lindy and I to wear the same uniform as the other nurses.

This is a long sleeved white jacket, not unlike a chef's jacket that is paired with very baggy white pull-on pants. The main thrust of my motivation regards the inability to perform CPR in our present stiff skirt. I also point out that it may be possible that the skirt rides up when demonstrating CPR, inadvertently exposing an ankle. I push the point home by adding that my husband would not be happy to have my ankles exposed to strangers. Dr. Mahir Al-Hassan calls me in to discuss the possibility of this suggestion (changing uniform, not exposing my ankles!) He says he agrees in principle with the idea but it may take a few days to get the Programme Director's final approval. I commend him on his ability to get things done and he has a quick preen, turning directly from his chair to face his glass cabinet, whose surface is so shiny it acts as a mirror. Dr. Al-Hassan is fond of addressing his reflection and constantly speaks to his image, adjusting his array of vibrant ties and tidying away any stray hairs from his impeccable head. In time we all become used to speaking to the reflection in the cabinet.

Lindy and I are both feeling very tired and listless. We decide to visit Dr. Faziem, the staff GP, for some vitamins. We go in together, as the doctor's reputation precedes him. For some odd reason I am given another *bataga* by the receptionist with a different number and silently ponder who is going to be charged for my nightmare filling of last week. We explain our need for vitamins. He immediately asks Lindy to open her blouse, as he needs to examine her chest.

"It's not necessary to examine my breasts doctor, I'm just tired, my breasts are fine!" she exclaims archly. He drops his stethoscope reluctantly and I stifle a giggle at his obvious disappointment. He refuses to give us vitamin C.

"Latest research states that vitamin C in large doses is dangerous!"

I politely ask him where he has read this research and try to contain my surprise when he says he saw it on the news last month! We leave clutching only a packet of vitamin B tablets!

Lindy and I decide to spend half an hour in the library, sitting on the only two chairs that are provided for females. They are situated behind a large screen in case a male doctor might also need to read some books and get distracted by female presence—vicariously or otherwise! In any event we are chucked out at prayer time.

Lindy gives me a hideous pink gilt plastic alarm clock in the shape of a mosque as a present. I love it. The alarm emits the first few bars of the ubiquitous call to prayer. We become very good at singing along to the loudspeaker at prayer time. It is somewhat disconcerting to be concentrating on something, to suddenly hear the first eerie loud wails of *Allah Akbar* rent the air.

Col, Tim and I decide to visit the El-Rashid shopping centre in town. It's very big with lots of glitz and glitter. We find an entertainment centre within its walls and Tim is off. There are bumper cars, *flying* planes and something akin to a small Ratanga junction in Cape Town, with a train on wheels. Many Riyals' part hands as Tim, and later

Col and I, partake of a ride or two! I need a cup of tea and we find a pleasant looking garden café with a pretty view of flowers and bushes. We sit at one of the tables but are told this area is for (privileged) single males only; the married section is behind closed doors with absolutely no view or atmosphere. We have a very expensive cup of coffee and a slice of cheesecake while gazing around the bare beige walls. I am still drinking my very hot tea when suddenly the waiter approaches us.

"It is prayer time Madame," he informs me. I nod in assent. I too can hear the piercing call of the muezzin.

"No, no, Madame. You not understand," exclaims the waiter in agitation,

"It is prayer time, you must go!" He flaps a slim brown hand towards the door. I am annoyed. I feel dehydrated and am about to rehydrate which means I need my tea.

"I will first drink my tea," I explain as pleasantly as possible "Then I will leave and go outside.'

The waiter wrings his hands in consternation, "Madame, you MUST go now, please!" He will be in big trouble from the *muttawan* should I be caught drinking during prayer time. My decision is made; I pick up the tray with the pot of tea, jug of milk and cup and move to the door. The waiter stands staring at me in amazement, but wisely does not try to stop me. I leave with Col and Tim and position myself on the dirty cracked pavement steps outside the café with my tray of tea, setting it down carefully before topping up my cup. I notice a twitch of lace from the café window and the bewildered face of the waiter peers briefly out at me. Tim and Col are laughing on the steps beside me. Now, however, we are committed to the blazing hot sun, thick work clothing and a cup of hot tea, sweating profusely while the locals scurry around en route to their place of prayer.

Later *Bictor* and Astor tell me there are female Muttawan! They dress all in black, including gloves and headgear.

This is interesting and I think back to the black dressed harridan I'd met at the airport and surmise she must have been one. No male, other than the husband or other family member, may touch a Saudi women. So the female *Muttawan* are given this task.

We're still feeling very tired. I suspect the air conditioner; the bright light and the clock are all to blame. Despite this Lindy and I decide to move our office furniture around. For some reason this burst of activity unleashes a fit of giggling that lasts most of the day. Even when Sue informs us that there's a rumour going around that we aren't getting paid this month, we don't let up, and in fact giggle even more. I later attribute this to extreme anxiety but at that moment our reaction does nothing for our reputation and Sue backs off and hurries down the corridor. Victor peers in a short while later and is surprised to the see two senior members of staff hurling heavy furniture around the room and laughing uncontrollably.

At home I begin work on an email message home when the spacebar character disappears.

"Oh no! God! Where has it gone?"

Panicking, I press several keys but the screen remains devoid of toolbars

"What am I going to tell Colin? He'll kill me!"

I am learning this computer business as I go along and in fact have devised a system of using *post its* to write down the basic functions. 'Switch on computer with knob thingy on left hand side of screen' directs one pink post-it stuck in the vicinity of the screen.

"Lindy, thank heavens you're home, I've gone and buggered up the computer. It's just not working." She promises to phone around the Corniche centre and see if anyone can offer advice. I haven't explained the real problem to her out of embarrassment at my lack of IT knowledge. I am already in bed when the phone rings. It's someone called Anthony. He works in IT at the university and he offers to help me with my computer problem. Groping around in the dark I find the light switch. It is 11:15pm.

"Hi, sorry for bothering you," I begin somewhat inadequately. "I was busy writing an email when suddenly; boom! It wasn't there—the toolbar—I mean."

There is a silence.

"The tool bar?"

"Yes, that thing at the bottom of the screen without which I can't do a thing!" Anthony coughs slightly then patiently takes me through some simple steps, when suddenly, everything goes dark—screen, room, fax machine—all are as dead as a dodo.

"Hello, Anthony, can you hear me?" I cry into the phone. There is no response and I sit in the dark wondering what to do next. Ten minutes later Anthony manages to phone me just as I'm climbing back into bed, the computer whirrs into life although the lights are still off so we continue with the repair job in torchlight. After some minutes, Anthony has rescued my computer desktop and the spacebar sits down at the bottom where it's meant to be. All is again well with the technical world as I am beginning to know it.

"Thank you so much." I burble gratefully and hang up, then head once again to my bed. The lights suddenly flood the room and I stagger out of bed again to switch them off.

Col comes in ten minutes later and I sleepily tell him I've sorted out the computer problem. He says he didn't think we had one but gets a snore in response.

CHAPTER SIX

"If you reject the food, ignore the customs, fear the religion and avoid the people, you might better stay at home."

James Michener

The Mannequins of Shula

MY IQAMA ARRIVED today. To receive one so soon (after only 25 days) is virtually unheard of. Normally there is a three month probation period, so I am feeling rather pleased with myself. As I walk back to the Education department clutching my prize, I pass the male waiting room where groups of men are sitting or standing and chatting between themselves. I think they look smart and regal in their traditional dress.

Men and boys wear the *thobe*, an ankle length garment which fits loosely to the ground. Although the *thobe* covers almost the entire body, the loose design allows for air to circulate freely. It is normally made from a white cotton material (specially in summer) in stark contrast to the heavier, dark coloured *abaya* that the females are forced to wear. Men also wear a *ghutra,* a square head cloth of either plain or pink chequered cloth. This piece of clothing, which is folded into a triangle, was traditionally made of cotton. A small white skullcap called a *tagia* lies underneath the ghutra. The *igal*, a double circle of black rope or cord, holds the *ghutra* on the head.

Staying with heads and tradition for a minute, Victor tells me about the last beheading they had here in Al-Khyber. It was apparently only two months ago and I am horrified to hear it still happens. He says all the locals pack a picnic basket and head for the city centre where the beheading takes place. Imagine tucking into a cheese sandwich while some poor individual loses his head. It's archaic and incomprehensible to me in this century. The reasoning behind the open invitation to watch is to set an example. I guess it works.

Lindy and I are excited when we have a computer delivered to our office. Lindy had asked Dr. Al-Hammad for one a few weeks ago. Ding sets it down carefully (on Lindy's desk) He plugs it in and starts it up. We both peer expectantly at the brightening blue screen.

"Well it's not exactly Windows 98, more like 68!" I exclaim in disappointment.

This machine is not much better than an electric typewriter. Lindy vows to motivate for a more updated computer soon. Astor tries to be helpful when he passes by. He looks over and says,

"Hmmm. I *theenk* you need to get some more *flobby biskettes por* the computer *piles*." Lindy looks over at me and bites her lip.

"Thanks Astor."

"Sixty people killed!" screams the headlines. I pause to take a sip of tea and read further.

The huge wedding tent that burned down yesterday in Riyadh has killed over sixty people and injured hundreds more. It is mostly women and children who are burned to death. This is most likely because they are segregated from the males. It is thought that a hubbly-bubbly pipe fell over and started the fire. I wonder about the effects of the strict segregation laws here.

If more men had been present I'm sure they would have been able to help the terrified women and children.

Trevor, from the dive club, sets up his laptop on our table and shows us an amazing sequence of events. We're sipping cold lagers at Al-Razza compound around a clear blue pool.

"Just look at this mate," says Trevor, taking a sip of his beer and moving the mouse around the screen. We both move closer. Just before Tim and I arrived in Saudi there was a large shopping centre called the Al-Shuma. It was very popular with Westerners and locals alike.

Apparently you could buy almost anything there and the prices were good.

A week before we got here there was a fire at the Shuma. Maybe faulty wiring, no-one is sure but as the fire increased in volume and intensity, the shopkeepers were seen frantically grabbing all they could from their shops and rushing out of the centre.

"No-one wanted to phone the fire department because the unwritten rule in Saudi is, whoever phones about a fire is held responsible, and naturally no-one was too keen on that,"

Trevor says,

"So the flames rose higher and higher. Eventually, some chap who lived in an apartment nearby, telephoned the fire department, situated literally just across the way.

They arrived after another twenty minutes." The story goes that they were trying to find the keys for the fire engines!

"My pal Dave lived in the apartment and was filming the sequence of events from his window." Trevor chuckles wryly.

"He sees only one fire engine pull up outside the burning Shuma and watches as two firemen hop out of the vehicle with a ladder." Trevor leans forward to add intrigue.

"Dave notices that none of them are wearing oxygen masks or cylinders. They put the ladder against the front wall and the other fellow unravels a water hose. He climbs the ladder and water flows out of the hose in a single useless jet. People are trapped in the lift but these two are playing with the water!"

He tells us that a few minutes later another fire engine arrives and another couple of firemen shuffle out. Men are seen rushing out of the Shuma with mannequins, all of which have been hastily covered in some piece of clothing, grabbed in passing, so as not to offend the Saudi's.

What presence of mind in an emergency or perhaps a more sinister illustration of the Sharia fear under which these people live every day. Trevor shows us the photographs that were taken by this friend of his. The last in the sequence is truly amazing and describes the Saudi mindset to a 'T'. As we peer closer to the screen we see what Trevor's forefinger is pointing to. Three firemen are seen kneeling down on the ground facing *away* from the burning building.

"It's prayer time you see." explains Trevor while we look on incredulously.

Yes, it is true. The firemen, knowing it is prayer time, dutifully kneel facing Mecca while this huge building blazes on and sixty people are burned to death. It took three days to extinguish the fire and all that remains is a charcoal shell of a once popular shopping centre.

I shake my head and take a large gulp of watery beer.

A few weeks after working at the hospital they decide to give Lindy and I an orientation!

We have been working here long enough to receive this news with equanimity and meet in the auditorium to join a Saudi psychologist from USA, Jubie from South Africa and Miriam from Ghana.

Ruth opens the lecture with a talk on infection control principles (information outdated and incorrect.)

Leanne informs us what she expects of her staff and a round Egyptian woman in long dress and veil called *Mama Houd* opens her speech by telling us her daughter is a Muttawa.

"My daughter, Ashara, she must teach the young boys how to pee sitting down so that the evil spirits don't get into the toilet bowel."

She guffaws loudly at the surprised expressions on our faces.

"In Sharia law, there must be one male or two females present for meetings, this is in case one of the females is menstruating in which case her statement will be thought '*unreliable*'!

I am aghast at such blatant sexist thinking. She also says interestingly that the rule about women having to be covered up is a man—made law and has nothing to do with Islam. I had figured as much!

It's a pity the millions of women who are covered from head to foot in unbearable temperatures haven't '*cottoned on!*'

Back in the apartment Colin has brought Chuck, a friend from work, to help find the m*y computer* icon on our desktop. It disappeared early yesterday morning and hasn't been seen since. Chuck seems amused at the request and it isn't long before he retrieves this icon from wherever these things go to hide. I tell them both about the orientation and Mama Houd.

They don't seem as put out about the 'two woman per meeting' rule as I am which miffs me somewhat.

Dr. Al-Hammad offers Lindy and I a cream bun this morning. He steals a few appreciative glances at his reflection as we sit nibbling on the cake and chatting about how quickly time is passing (true) and much work we've accomplished (not true) Dr. H straightens his tie and steals another quick glance at his office cabinet and murmurs that he is pleased with *his girls*.

Lindy and I preen and lick cream off our fingers and gaze at him attentively as he emphasizes the importance of maintaining the image of 'his' department.

I witness a *Code Blue* today. I'm in Male med talking to Cathy when the loudspeaker goes off and a crackly voice calls, "code blue, code blue in ward three!" I follow Cathy into a cramped cubicle where an ineffectual chest compression is taking place by a Filipina nurse using only two fingers I try to intervene, but the nurse manager, Al-Katani in her flowing white robes pushes me out of the way and takes over. The patient dies! I am so cross I storm out of the room leaving her to call for *lay out*.

Back in the office I grumble to Lindy;

"What's the point in hiring an educator to ensure the latest techniques if they just want to stay in the dark ages!" Lindy murmurs in sympathy but she is writing up her ICU lecture. It is a week overdue.

Dr. H calls me in to his office and asks about my leave.

"Uh, I need about five days."

"*Thees* is impossible!" His eyes twitch when I say my husband will be very angry with me if I don't get the leave.

"He would love to meet you Dr. Hammad." I quickly continue, "I've spoken so highly of you and you are both in the same profession. He knows how difficult it is!" I say.

Dr. Al-Hammad turns to the shiny cupboard for confirmation then fingers his bright yellow tie.

" I am a fair man," he says, lowering his eyes modestly,

" I will speak with your husband and see . . ."

We don't get a chance to see what he would see because his cell phone rings. He speaks rapidly in Arabic while I wait politely for him to finish. Then suddenly both phones on his desk ring simultaneously. He ends the cell phone conversation, picks up the other two phones, holding one at each ear and chatters to each caller.

"I'm just doing my *butt.*" He says in between the Arabic. I bite down on my lip. It is when the cell phone rings again and he lowers his face to the table in order to speak into it, still holding a phone at each ear, that I decide to leave, collapse in my office and laugh till tears come to my eyes.

Our taxi driver looks about twelve years old. Lindy directs him to the Corniche centre. His feet do manage to reach the pedals though, which is reassuring and he drives fairly slowly.

Lindy's apartment is very similar to my own at the Corniche, small and not very welcoming.

It is very sparsely furnished, just a bed and small sideboard, one sofa and two pale beige armchairs in the lounge and a small round dining table.

She takes me to the pool deck which is on the rooftop. It has a good view of Al-Khyber.

I can see the Gulf Sea to the right and the *corniche* stretching along the sea for a few kilometres.

Corniche in Arabic generally refers to a piece of land that juts out from the main land, usually bordered by water.

"One tea and one coffee please." The waiter in the restaurant on the ground floor of the Corniche centre takes our order for drinks. For a smile he brings us a free mango juice as well.

"*Shukran.*"

"Eugh!" Lindy grimaces as she takes a sip, "Sugar!" We are somewhat surprised to receive two more cups of tea and coffee as soon as we've finished the first two cups and the mango juice.

The proprietor comes up to us with a huge smile. He hands us his card with a flourish and stands watching us as we take more sips of the ghastly hot sweet brew. He smiles encouragingly at us while my bladder fills up rapidly. It's a great relief when Col and Tim arrive!

"Bye Lindy, we must do tea again sometime!" She laughs and heads towards the lift.

I need to change out of my work clothes. My apartment still smells damp and musty, the carpet is still wet and the sheets are mysteriously missing off my bed. The kitchen floor suddenly oozes soapy suds from a hole in the floor! On our way down we meet a surly security guard who tells Col he is not allowed in my room. I tell him he's my husband, but it makes no difference to this man, who sighs as though he's heard it all before.

"You sign sleep over form next time." he says. I tell him Col isn't sleeping over, and only stayed fifteen minutes anyway but he's not interested. Col then tells him about the terrible condition of the room and the kitchen floor. This just means we have even more forms to fill in!

We pass a group of Arab males wearing their Friday best and a cloud of perfume.

They are returning from the mosque where they presumably asphyxiated the rest of the crowd.

Arabian men love perfume and it is something of an amusement to see the male patients in hospital receiving flowers and perfume. The women however don't usually get any.

Today Col accompanies me to my hospital. He meets Dr. Al-Hammad who ushers us both, and then Lindy for some reason, into his small office. The three of us perch uncomfortably on his hard chairs and receive the obligatory juice and tissue. The chat lasts almost forty five minutes and includes everything but the real reason we are there—to ask that I may be granted five days leave. Dr. H is in top form and conversation is peppered with, *doing my butts* and how he hates to *squeeze people*, each statement said with a quick glance at his reflection. Even Col ends up talking to the cupboard.

Conversation ends on a fairly positive note however with Dr. H ushering us out with the words,

"I am a fair man."

Out of the blue I end up being given the job of redesigning the entire AV department!

"How the hell did that happen!" Lindy just smiles, "you dared to ask for leave."

We decide to go shopping after work. After entering the souqs Lindy bargains for a watch. She manages to get it for SR25. It is worth at least double that! She's very good at bargaining and also walks the street with a skill that would be the envy of any New Yorker, dodging expertly between moving vehicles, stopping other cars with a raised hand. I'm not that lucky. They're more likely to run me over than stop when I lift my hand! I've heard from Hala, Delia's secretary that it is because of my red hair.

"I'm a witch you see. An evil woman! Har har!" Hala is not amused.

Colin meets up with me later to cash in my first salary cheque. Saudi-Hollandi Bank is a small open plan bank specially catering for men and Western women.

Standing patiently in line for my turn is easy when there's some pecuniary reward at the end of it. I hand over my cheque and wait for the cash. Instead of money, the bearded man in the white *thobe* and stiff chequered *ghutra* returns my cheque.

"There's no money." The teller states simply.

He looks past me for the next person in line. I hold up my hand,

"Wait a minute, what do you mean there's no money?" I slide my rejected cheque over to him again,

"You don't understand, this is my *salary* cheque." Speaking slowly as though his lack of English is the problem. He shrugs and passes the offending cheque back over the counter.

"There is no money to cover the funds. No money in this account," Now it's his turn to speak slowly and clearly to me. I turn away numb with shock. All my working life, since seventeen years of age, I have never had my salary cheque bounce before. Col and I walk along the cracked pavements in a daze. He has just transferred his entire income to our offshore bank account and the rest had to pay for Tim's school fees. We are to have lived off my pay this month. Feeling dejected, we go off for a quick bite. The burger is as tasteless as my cheque would have been had I eaten it instead.

The next morning, I'm dropped off at the hospital and I prepare to do battle. Pay Roll department shrug their collective shoulder and avert their eyes when I ask where my money is. After taking a deep breath I ask the Saudi who has his head down, his *ghutra* carefully concealing his features, the name of his boss. He looks up in surprise, maybe this one isn't going to go away quietly, he's probably thinking.

"You can speak with Mr. Majiet," he says.

"What time does he come to work?"

He says his hours are from 8am till 4pm. My watch says it is now 09H20 so I stomp off in the direction of his office. He isn't there. Nor is he there at various intervals over the next two hours. I finally get him in at 12:40. Majiet wears a *thobe, ghutra and igal.* He is sitting at his huge polished walnut desk sipping cardamom coffee. He eyes me over his gold-rimmed coffee glass,

"How may I be of assistance?" he enquires taking a sip.

"I was embarrassed at the bank yesterday," I begin, "I was embarrassed and surprised when my salary cheque was not honoured." Majiet takes another sip of coffee then carefully sets the small glass down. He looks at me with a hint of sympathy.

"I apologize for this. I promise you that your money will be in the bank today or tomorrow." I feel hopeful but turning to leave he utters the words that send me back to despair,

"*Ins'Allah.*" I close the door behind me and my shoulders slump. "*Ins'Allah*!" He may as well have said '*never*!' The word is tacked to the end of any verbal promise and removes all responsibility from the bearer with the result that any effort required to ensure that the promise bears fruit, is rarely made.

I Help Lindy finish off the CPR assessments. We sit on the steps of the Education department marking papers and eating cheese salad rolls. There is an eclipse today. Everyone wanders around with a piece of X-ray paper over their eyes gazing up at the darkening sun. Ignoring the eclipse, I decide to phone Majiet again and keep phoning until 4pm, then give up. The solar eclipse shows around 70-80% in Saudi today. Majiet is just a *total* eclipse!

The following day Lindy accompanies me to Personnel to make a nuisance of ourselves. Persistence is key. I call it the mosquito effect; persistent whining until blood is drawn! We speak to the vice captain. He *can't believe* I haven't been paid yet. He hands me a date wrapped in a tissue and says we must go and see the Captain of the Hospital.

We find him sitting behind a lavish wooden desk. You can always tell how important someone in Saudi is by the size of his name plaque. This one is made from dark polished wood with intricate calligraphy spelling out his typically long name and position. It covers 90% of the desk, with the legend: *Mohammed Bin al-Fatini captain; King Waheed Airbase Hospital*.

Captain Al-Fatini glances up from his newspaper and waits for me to state my purpose. When I finish he coughs at length into a paper tissue from the flowery box on his desk, and says I am not the only one that has not received payment. Oh, there are others? Sorry for asking, that makes all the difference to know there are other poor sods like me who have worked all month and now have nothing to show for it. What I actually say is,

"Yes many are unhappy. Can I tell them there is positive news to impart?" (You start to talk funny after a while in Saudi, something to do with their love of antiquated flowery language) Captain Fatini clearly couldn't give a stuffed date how many others are affected. He tells me to speak with Majiet, and returns to his newspaper. I'm dismissed.

Dejectedly I walk over to the Personnel building and look for Majiet. He isn't there. He doesn't answer his phone either when I call later. I meet Mel in the female cafeteria and she says he's not coming in. I bite back a scream and choose a cream donut instead.

Delia is wearing the same uniform we were wearing until recently and she sits behind her busy looking desk, fanning herself in the heat,

"It was 53° C on Friday," she says, getting up to put on the kettle,

"We nearly died in the heat. Sugar?" she enquires. Lindy nods. Delia makes us coffee off the top of her filing cabinet. As we sit sipping it through pursed lips, Delia regales us with stories of her ex-boss in Riyadh.

"I wasn't allowed to speak in meetings and, as a mere woman, I had to stand". We raise our eyes in disbelief.

"If he couldn't find a file," she continues, "even if it was staring him right in the face, I had to surreptitiously indicate to him where it was without him losing face." She sighs and takes a gulp of coffee. "I *hadda* leave the room if they spoke about things like abortion or pregnancy."

Delia tells us, in her characteristic Canadian drawl, of a Saudi man in Jeddah who wanted to marry a beautiful ten-year-old girl, the daughter of his friend. Women are generally covered from the age of eleven or twelve, especially once they have started menstruating. This man became impatient waiting for her to start her period and decides to have her see a gynaecologist to *hasten* matters along! It wasn't long before he marries her and by twelve years old she is pregnant!

"Hateful custom!" we agree in unison.

There are five female Saudi's for in-service. They are all doctors and they are all veiled. I seat them on plastic chairs in the AV room and put the CPR video on for them to watch while overseeing the installation of our new white cupboards, which Ding has brought in.

A termite mound is revealed on the floor while moving furniture around. Ding hurries into the office as I'm trying to clean it up with a few tissues.

"You *mus'* not *poot* the Saudi ladies alone in the room with us!" he exclaims in outraged whispers.

"What?"

He explains that unrelated males are not allowed to be in a room alone with Saudi women. He says he has placed a screen across the area from his desk. He rushes back and I leave the cupboards and termite mounds reluctantly, returning to find my group of Saudi female doctors still avidly watching the end of the video. Ding sits in his small closed space behind the screen. Their honour remains intact. I sigh, switch off the video and turn brightly to face my small, as yet unidentifiable audience, and tell them they are about to put some CPR into practice. A short while later I sit back in my chair and sigh again,

"They were hopeless." I tell Lindy who is tapping away on her computer.

"Who are?" she asks turning towards me.

"Those Saudi doctors!" I reply slamming down the CPR reports I'd just finished marking.

"They refuse to go anywhere near the male CPR doll. Dunno how on earth I'm supposed to assess someone on life saving if they hover above them fully veiled like some kind of black butterfly!" As the men are not allowed to touch a female who is not his wife, and vice versa the idea they can even *try* and perform CPR is doomed from the start.

I'd heard the other day in the canteen that in an accident, especially one where Westerners are involved, the Westerner will always be at fault. Their reasoning is simple; at least to the local way of thinking, the accident would never have happened if the Westerner hadn't been there in the first place!

A Land of lost logic as Tom would say!

I accompany Lindy to the payroll office to see if Dr. Al-Fahad can get her a salary advance. We are told to sit down and wait as he's on the phone. We do so and look around his lushly furnished office waiting for him to finish. When he does, another uniformed Saudi official enters the office and starts the complicated Arabic ritual of greeting; kissing each other's cheek and enquiring after the other's health before stating the purpose for his visit. Ten more minutes of chatting and he leaves, only to have someone else come in and the process begins again. The air is thick with the smell of heavy perfume. Lindy and I are ignored. Suddenly the absurdity of the situation hits us and we get a giggling fit. I leave the office for a minute to compose myself after another visitor brings the good doctor a huge bunch of flowers and the kissing ritual commences once again. When I return, Lindy, who is now sitting in front of Al-Fahad, is informing him that she has come to him as a last resort for an advance on her salary. I sit down next to her and nearly fall off the chair when she says she needs the money for her children's teeth and eyes.

"They all have poor eyesight and terrible teeth." her chin trembles with emotion (or suppressed laughter, I wasn't sure which). Dr. Al-Fahad looks at her for a moment then reaches into the folds of his *thobe*. I have an anxious moment but he merely draws his dark leather wallet out, opens it and extracts two neatly folded SR 500 bills and hands them to Lindy, who is uncharacteristically silent. When she finds her voice she thanks him over and over for his kindness.

"My children will hold you in their prayers for ever," she declares a bit dramatically. It is only SR1000 after all. He smiles and makes her sign a piece of paper to the effect that he has loaned her this money. Lindy stands and thanks him effusively again. He nods then his eyes fall on me, still sitting in astonishment.

"Do you need some money as well?"

I shake my head, "No, no thanks." He looks expectantly at me so I continue,

"I just wanted to say thank you so much for giving me my salary." He beams at me.

"You're welcome."

Tim has a variety show lined up for us when we get in.

"Come mummy and daddy," he says, grasping each of our hands in his. He leads us from the kitchen to the lounge and sits us down on the turd-coloured sofa. He has a karate show in line for us this evening followed immediately by a magic show. Just as we think it's over Tim enters the room as a ninja wearing some underpants over his pyjamas and brandishing bits of his toy railway track. I smile and clap enthusiastically but I'm thinking we need to get him some more friends.

Lindy and I are called into Dr. Al-Hammad's office. The smell of cardamom with a hint of saffron assails the nose as we enter. This morning we are given cardamom coffee in tiny cups. I sip slowly and enjoy its pungent rich taste but can tell Lindy isn't enjoying hers. Doctor H opens the meeting by saying we must all do our *butt* and here his eyelids close slightly, his lips purse and I pause mid sip. This twitch of his usually precedes something he doesn't like to talk about.

"I'm an honourable man," he begins, with a quick glance at his honourable reflection. This reassures him sufficiently to continue.

"But I cannot allow you both to work overtime."

Ah! there it is. The reason for the coffee. Lindy looks disappointed but I have no intention of working overtime.

"The General will not allow this." continues Dr. H. He quickly turns and reaches down into the small fridge beside him to extract two small cans of frozen fruit juice, wraps each can in tissue paper and hands one to each of us.

I shove mine quickly into my trouser pocket where it gently freezes my thigh. I take another sip of coffee.

"I'm sorry but this is not my decision." He turns to his reflection and closes his eyes again for a moment. The discussion is over and I gulp down the remainder of my coffee and set the tiny cup down on his desk. My frozen thigh impedes a fast exit. As we leave his office Lindy whispers to me,

"Don't worry, there's another way."

I look up questioningly.

"Blood!" she says, enigmatically taking a sip of her juice. I am instantly relieved to hear she means donating it rather than spilling it in any way.

"Apparently they pay westerners good dough to donate blood." Lindy thinks this is the answer to her financial problems. I'm . . . not so sure!

Chapter Seven

"There are no foreign lands. It is the traveler only who is foreign."

Robert Louis Stevenson

Hashing in the kingdom

Col arrives to collect me at around 4:30. As usual my sunglasses have misted over as I step outside and I nearly walk into the car door. We drive to the nearby centre for a spot of shopping. Col leaves Tim and I in the shopping centre while he drives off to find a photography shop on the other side of town. We're standing outside a toyshop when, without warning, the lights go out and Salah—prayer time, begins.

"Look mummy," Tim points excitedly at a small wooden airplane in the toyshop window. The shop lights are still on so we walk in.

"Hello. How much is that little plane in the window?" (sung to the tune of, 'how much is that doggy in the window, the one with the waggly tail').

The Pakistani shopkeeper and I are in the middle of bargaining it down from SR20 to SR15 when an apparition in a short white *thobe* and scraggly red beard casts a dark shadow at the door. His headgear is missing an *iqal* and he's pointing a shaking hennaed finger at me shouting something unintelligible in Arabic. He approaches and says hysterically,

"Cover up, cover up!"

He is almost frothing at the mouth. The uniformed figure standing just behind the irate man with the long stick informs me that this is a Muttawa, the religious police against vice. He is not the nice, kind Muttawa that we have at the hospital. This one means business!

"Cover hair!" His eyes bulge with indignation.

He is incensed that we are flouting two rules; wearing my loose hair uncovered as well as the fact we are in the shop purchasing something at prayer time. He advances further towards me, stick quivering in mock sympathy to the common cause.

While trying to tie my headscarf quickly over my head with shaking fingers his attention is momentarily distracted by the cowering shopkeeper who is whimpering behind the counter. The policeman, as reinforcement, steps up behind him as the Arabic diatribe continues in shrill crescendo. I grab Tim's hand and whisper fiercely,

"Come on, let's run!"

We're out of the door and along the top floor in a matter of seconds. I turn around as we reach the other side.

"Oh Heck, they're coming!" This is when I hear a sharp *"Psst!"* I look round and a disembodied hand beckons us from behind a door. The hand belongs to a Jordanian coffee shop owner. His shop displays the legend, *Al-Jeer best coffee*. The door opens and we are quickly ushered inside its darkened interior. I glance through the net-curtained window and see the Muttawa and police escort if not running, then certainly moving very quickly past. I breathe a sigh of relief and thank our rescuer.

"These Muttawan are a problem in the shopping centre's here in Khyber. They chase away business." I nod sympathetically. We remain safely behind the door of the coffee shop until prayer time ends, drinking hot Arabic coffee.

I tell Col about our Muttawa experience while having supper at Babba Habbas later that evening.

"I told you; always keep your head covered at prayer times," advises Colin who doesn't have to put more than hair gel on *his* head!

Rehaad is dressed in a very smart shirt and tie this morning but Dr. H in contrast has his local gear on. It is strange seeing him in the Arabic dress of *thobe, iqal and ghutra*. We've become used to the smart Western dress. Not that he isn't now as neat as always, it's just the contrast between a flowing sheet and a Saville row suit!

We discuss the Y2K thing in the policy meeting today. Everyone seems to think we are all going to have a huge problem. I don't really know enough about it to form an opinion but I do know I'm not going to be stock-piling any candles and tinned meat any time soon.

Delia tells me that Tim, as my son, should have spoken up for me when confronted by the Muttawa! I can hardly believe he would have listened to a six year old but Delia says he would. I think Tim is already taking on far too many typically male traits. He and Col marched ten paces ahead of me through our apartment swing doors the other day, leaving me to stagger behind them laden down with shopping!

"Ah. Jhanette," Rehaad beams at me as I'm passing his office.

"It would be a great honour if you are able to assist me with *somsing.*"

"What?" I ask him suspiciously,

"Please just help me by reading this *arteekle* which has been written by the honourable doctor Al Zaid."

"and . . . ?"

"Just read it," he begs, "and if it *eez* possible please make the adjustments to it as you see fit."

"Why?" Rehaad loses eye contact for a second,

"Um, *eet* is to assist *heem wiz heez arteekle* for publication,"

"So you want me to read this doc's article, correct any spelling mistakes and give it back for publishing?"

"Thank you Jhanette, God will reward you."

I take a look. It describes pressure sores and is not very good. It's like reading a grade 10 homework essay! I place several hundred red lines through the work and rewrite most of it. I return the article the next day. Rehaad is sitting with someone in his office. There's no introduction, so nodding slightly at the silent man in full local dress, I hand the article over to Rehaad, who asks me if I needed to make any corrections.

"Well, my pencil was a lot longer when I started!"

He laughs, takes the article and hands it to the man sitting next to him.

"Here is your *arteekle* for the journal of medicine Dr. Al-Zaid. *Jhanette* has corrected all your *meestakes,*" he says with a wicked smile.

The doctor does not look too put out but I am furious. "Rehaad, that is not very kind of you," turning to the writer I say somewhat insincerely that I had really enjoyed reading the article and mumble my apologies. I leave with Rehaad's laughter ringing in my ears.

The Saudi Hash territory

"On, On! Come on lads and lassies!"

It's *Hash* day today. My first one in Saudi, actually my first ever! We are following other *hounds by* means of white powdery arrows around a large pale yellow dune. We were introduced to the Hash way of life an hour earlier.

Most of our group is wearing the Al-Khyber Hash Harrier T-shirts in lurid yellow. Lindy, Big and little Sue are there as well as my *roommate* from the Corniche, Louise. Sue, at fifty plus, is the group leader who takes us through the rules of the hash in a thick Geordie accent. She is wearing white frilly shorts that barely cover her bottom. She has nice legs though. She bellows some hash rules to the large group from the back of a pick up. Judging from the general lack of attention, most of the people here have heard it all before but *I* am hanging onto every word. I hear something about following the flour or is it flower? Anyway suddenly everyone takes off towards the dunes following some dude blowing a bugle. I find it too hot to run and slow down to a gentle trot. My bladder is full and I find a short bush to pee behind. As I'm crouching over the hot sand I see a small pale lizard dart by and reflect that I have seen precious little else in terms of wild life since coming to Saudi Arabia. Actually I have to eat my words a few minutes later because a small herd of pale orange coloured camels come rocking by led by the—Pakistani—herdsman. I find it strange that they don't have many local Arabian herdsmen anymore.

Hashing originated in Kuala Lumpur in 1938 by Thomson, Lee, and A S Gispert, a group of British officers and expatriates who started their own club after the traditional *Hare and Hounds*, an activity that was supposed to keep members of the club fit in between bouts of drinking and eating and general overindulgence.

So what happens is, pack of hounds *(runners)* chase down the trail set by the hare or hares *(other runners)* who set trails of arrows and circles in flour, after which both hares and hounds gather together for a bit of social activity known as the *Down Down* with mock trials for some made up on the spot mild misdemeanor. Refreshment follows the trials in the form of *white or red paint* (wine) and weak home made beer, humour, song and a braai (BBQ) close the proceedings. Hashing now takes place all over the world.

The *down down* takes place after the run while we're all cooling off. Lindy has to finish a cup of weak frothy beer while we all sing, '*down, down*.' The court *hearing* has found her guilty. Her transgression is apparently messing with Sue's camera before the start!

"And the following three have been found guilty of being virgins. Come up Colin, Jan and Tim!"

My smile disappears as we walk to the front. *Virgins* (the hash term for newcomers) are not exempt it would seem! We are handed a full mug of watery brew to slug back. I'm relieved to see that Tim is given a Fanta to drink. We lift our arms and swig down our respective beverages to the loud chants of *Drink it down, down!*

It's dusk and we've slipped under the barbed wire fence of the compound after depositing Tim in his bed. We walk away from the hospital buildings in the waning light until it is almost dark save a pale moon. I am still very hot and sweaty so I eventually throw all caution to the wind (and reason too, given our location and lack of clothing underneath) and remove my *abaya*. A slight breeze cools us. Two sand lizards move quickly over the dune in a dash of pink and ochre. A couple of stray dogs run over the distant dunes close to a Bedouin settlement. We walk for twenty minutes more but don't see much else.

"Quite a successful afternoon's entertainment." I say slipping my *abaya* back over my head.

"I'll never quite work out the hash lot," returns Col, "but they do provide a great wine!"

"*Morneeng Jhanette*. You *weel* see Dr. Al Hammad —he *ees* in the Male Med ward"

"OK Raheed, I'll see him later after my lecture." thinking he means he is doing his rounds there. Rehaad frowns and shakes his head,

"No, he *ees eel*. He is admitted yesterday *weeth* the chest pain."

I look at him in alarm,

"Dr. H is sick? I'll go straight away and see him."

Lindy and I leave together to see D. Al-Hammad. We find him sitting up in bed looking pathetic and bored. It is strange seeing him normally so neat and tidy lying in bed wearing the hospital patterned pyjamas and ruffled hair.

"How are you?" I ask patting his hand tentatively, Saudi customs momentarily forgotten.

He shrugs, "I had the chest pain but I am much better and would like to leave now."

Lindy plumps up his pillows.

"You stay right there until they discharge you Dr. Hammad." she admonishes. We chat a few minutes longer and order him a milk drink. Debs finds us outside the ward and says he tried to discharge himself twice since yesterday.

"He's no *tae do annything rrisky but rrest*." she says in her broad Scottish accent.

"I'm that fed up wi' the bugger, I'll discharge him meself unless he starts to rrest." We laugh and say we know how she feels before returning to the education building. We have Aster draw us a card for Dr H. and ask the lads to sign it as well before dropping it off later.

Rehaad sells me some copper ornaments from Egypt today. They will do nicely as Christmas presents. We are planning to visit Col's mum in Sweden. While rushing down the corridor for a hurried lunch I pass several veiled women walking towards me and surprise myself by recognizing them variously by means of an arched eyebrow, a particular silhouette or by the type of shoe they wear! They are as pleased as I am when I greet them by name. I feel as though I've finally arrived and become part of the Saudi scene.

The next two days are spent rushing through hundreds of recerts and feeling slightly flu-ey. Lindy has a hectic weekend going to parties, bowls and the gym. She's enjoying herself and is looking good. The pounds are starting to drop off.

We're in the office when the phone rings, 'Hello? Education office.' All I can hear on the other end is a woman's shrill voice gabbling away in Arabic.

"Sorry no understand," I yell and put the phone down. A few minutes later the phone rings again. It's the same woman so I hand the phone to Lindy who takes her little English/Arabic dictionary out of the drawer. She reads the first sentence on page twelve in Arabic over the phone. What she's actually saying is, "please take a seat. The bus is late". Not sure if the woman on the other end understands but she doesn't phone again.

This morning Astor comes in looking anxious. There was a robbery in the hospital last night. Dr. H immediately has a huge iron security gate put up at the front door. He is on top form now that he's recovered. He chats to us in the corridor and ends with his trademark, 'All the best!' said with thumb raised. Big Sue visits us later and tells us that they have searched the Filipino quarters for the stolen computers. What a nerve! No wonder Astor and the boys were looking worried.

"My money's on a local," says big Sue. "By the way I'm fermenting my next twenty litres of red," she continues,

"Keeping it in the broom cupboard. I'll let you know when it's ready to drink."

We warn her to be careful but she just laughs and says she's been making the stuff for years. I order a bottle or two and recertify a Filipina from Peace Hawk called Jell Dell Marino. Another day in the life!

There is more talk about the Y2K bug today. Everyone reckons there will be a huge world wide problem, the computers will crash and no one in Saudi will be paid! What's new? Bring on the Millennium. John tells me he's entered an art competition to design the best Y2K millennium bug. My brother is good at that sort of thing.

We are all ushered out of the office at 4:10 by Astor and co. I'm slightly irritated as I'm in the middle of signing certificates. Only last week Dr. H was saying we must not leave before 4:30. My problem is that the taxi can't be summonsed at the last minute so I invariably end up sitting on the steps outside melting in the heat. At home Col has written a pile of emails to various people here and overseas. He presses the wrong button and sends his mum a copy of his tax returns. Nutter!

Dr. Al-Hammad won't sign approval for Lindy and I to have more than two uniforms. He says policy states that we may have only two. I tell him about the need for one in the wash, one on and one ready to wear.

"You wouldn't want your girls to look untidy in your department would you?" I ask digging the point in. Eventually he agrees and gives us permission. He's such a *woes* (pronounced woos, this is an Afrikaans word for a feeble spineless person). On my way to see Delia, I pass a Saudi man preening himself in the reflective glass for the emergency key, which hangs in the corridor. He adjusts his *ghutra* and turns this way and that. They are worse than the women I think as I pass. Oh right. I forgot. What would the women be looking at anyway, black gauze and eye slits! I reach the long 'L' shaped women's waiting room, which is full. One woman, who is totally covered, has a pair of spectacles perched somewhere in the region of her eyes. She has a baby on her lap gazing up in what I assume is a bewildered expression.

"Who is this woman?" I can almost hear it thinking as the black-gloved hands returns a dummy to its quivering mouth. Delia tells me that the children recognize their mothers by their shape, smell and the colour and design of their shoes and handbags. Amazing! I pause as if to check my notes and press the small button of my very basic digital camera hidden within its folds. I feel somewhat guilty doing this but there is no other way I could capture the scene before me.

Delia offers me some coffee or a pop and tells me a horrifying story of a Pakistani who entered Saudi with heroin sewn into his stomach. The authorities took him to their office to interrogate him. They have a dilemma. Where to behead him? for behead him they must.

"The usual place is too close to the holy mosque and might offend Allah! (or Mohammed PBUH)." Delia explains. The decision is made eventually by the Program Director. As a new recruit for the hospital in Tabuq, the man is taken there for an instant beheading in the hospital foyer using a large sharp surgical blade. The deed is done; the coroner is called down from his office to pronounce him dead and the body removed. The hospital's Western staff is abuzz with this awful impromptu activity of brutality regardless of his misdemeanour. Others would argue that it works.

I meet up with Lindy on the way back to the office and she says our salary cheques are in so we decide to order hospital transport into town. The driver drops us outside the bank and waits while we cash our respective cheques. He then takes us back to the education building. This is the first time I've ever had hospital transport take me to a bank to cash in my salary. We head back to our office with pockets bulging with Riyal notes sit behind our desks and begin to laugh. We laugh till our sides hurt but can't stop. This happens regularly these days and we both realize it's a sign of stress but once we start we just can't stop. If anyone comes in to talk to us, we just continue laughing. We must be offending a lot of people!

"Let's go to the linen department and get our clothes fixed," Suggests Lindy.

I nod, hoping it will sort out the excessive laughter. It doesn't! As we reach the huge front door to the *Linen Department*, we see another smaller door has been carved out of the larger one. Both have door handles and can be opened simultaneously. We start to giggle, debating which one to use. A notice pinned above the first handle says '*if you bang the door too hard you are liable for damages*'! In the end I decide to walk through the small door and Lindy enters the larger outer door. The effeminate dressmaker who minces over to us trailing his tape measure on the floor notes our simultaneous arrival with some surprise.

His Elvis styled hair has an exaggerated oiled quaff, which remains intact even as he moves.

"What can I do *por* you ladies?" he enquires with an arched eyebrow, hands on slim hips.

"Um, we need to change uniforms and have some trousers altered." I reply handing him my bundle. He takes the package and minces off. He returns and next minute he is on bended knee sporting a plethora of pins from his pursed lips, measuring my legs and thigh without managing to touch a cm of skin. He pins and tucks then straightens up.

"I *haf* fixed the pant. You can collect this next week." He sweeps a hand over his bouffant hair and walks off like a model with a carrot up the proverbial.

We both leave through the large door this time.

"I can't get over this place." says Lindy shaking her head.

Later I tell Hala about the imam who had passed wind rather loudly over the loudspeaker at the hospital yesterday whilst reciting the evening prayer. She is shocked, not because he'd farted but because the Koran does not allow this. Wow, go tell that to the chap who's just eaten a plate of foul beans (a staple here)

Col phones me mid morning to ask if Dr. al-Hammad will write a letter for his Egyptian *tryptique*, a customs permit, which serves as a passport for a motor vehicle.

In Saudi Arabia this includes a letter from a local businessman who will act as guarantor should anything go wrong. I corner Dr. H after prayer (a good time I think because he will be feeling pious), and ask if he knows of any Saudi business man who would sign this document so Col can take his car into Egypt. Dr. Al-Hammad immediately picks up one of his phones and prattles away for ten minutes in Arabic. He puts the phone down and looks at his cupboard, straightens his tie then gives me his attention. He says his friend will try and help Colin but he thinks the chap felt *squeezed* and he doesn't like *squeezing* people, this with a quick grimace at his reflection in the shiny cupboard image. I interject that I'm feeling pretty squeezed myself but my duty is to try and help my husband. I don't get much more out of him and plonk myself down at my desk sighing. Lindy says not to worry,

"I'll ask my friend, *good news* Irwin and see what he can come up with."

Lindy met Irwin, a Pakistani working in town, a few weeks ago in one of the electronic shops. He is besotted with her. Phones her at every opportunity. He likes to start with the words, "I have good news for you". If he can help Col get his *tryptique* I'll be happy and it will indeed be *good news!*

I decide to liven up the otherwise dull policy meeting a little this afternoon by recounting my day.

"Well this morning I started off by tumble drying half a dozen bread rolls,"

"Why?" They ask me.

"They were rolled up in a wet dish towel," I explain. Blank looks.

"I then burned Tim's toast to a black strip on the grill, got to work late and had a huge problem trying to video-tape the orientation lecture."

"Why?"

"Everything was too dark. The lighting was terrible, I could hardly see a thing!"

"What did you do?"

"I um, removed my sunglasses!"

They chuckle appreciatively then we turn our attention to, *Policy for assisting the patient to pray.* This is not as strange a title for a policy as it may sound. There are various conditions that have to be met during prayer time. Hospitalization can create a problem for patients, for example, when they are physically unable to prostrate themselves. In the case of immobility the patient may wish to pray in a sitting position in bed or nearby the bed on the ground on a clean area using their prayer mat. If no mat is available, a clean folded sheet can be used. Before prayer, the patient needs to perform ablution. [2] The ritual for washing normally takes the form of washing the hands; gargling and rinsing the mouth and nostrils, washing the

---

[2] Reference: en.wikipedia.org/wiki/Wudu

face, the arms, then passing wet hands over the hair and lastly washing the feet. A normal wash hand basin is adequate for performing the *Ablution* but they may need help if they are frail and elderly or weak. A jug of water and basin can also be used. Sometimes the patient may not use water for example if they have wounds, burns etc. The use of sterile sand or soil is permitted in these instances. For *Dry ablution*, as it is known, the patient lightly touches the soil with dry hands in a particular consecutive order. They must not be interrupted during the ritual. This policy takes us most of the afternoon to complete.

Chapter Eight

*I travel a lot; I hate having my life
disrupted by routine.*

Caskie Stinnett

Routines

We're sailing to Jubail this weekend. Tom leaves
first on a wooden dhow. It has an open wooden section at
the back that serves as the toilet seat. Everything goes into
a bucket. No thanks! Our dhow, although not as primitive,
hardly lives up to the glowing adjectives declared on their
advertisement. Our trip starts off inauspiciously enough.
We set our rucksacks and diving bags below decks and sit
in the small galley. The little wooden lifeboat is trailing
behind us on a rope. Soon afterwards, not more than half

an hour after setting off, the boat starts to rock from side to side like a cork, with huge swells that have come up suddenly.

"Damn! I've spilt my tea." Col stumbles against the deck rail. He glances down at Tim and me,

"Typical! The first time I bring you two we have bad sea conditions."

You'd think it was *our* fault! The usually still, calm gulf water is a churning mass. I can't even see through the front window with grey waves breaking over its greasy surface. Everything's awash with water. I start to feel a little green so shuffle to the edge of my seat and gently slide to the floor. The smell of diesel wafts up from below deck and I have to swallow several times as nausea takes over. I am nevertheless amused at the sight of everyone lurching around like drunkards. It's impossible to venture even two steps in a straight line. Some people are using a slightly shaky step forward and back like a chameleon, in an attempt to get to the other side of the boat. Looking up from the floor, the porthole shows a perpendicular skyline. Eventually we down anchor close to a small island. There is nothing there really but a sand dune in the ocean, with an ugly metal obelisk in the centre. I thought being anchored may help the nausea but the motion of the boat bobbing up and down keeps the queasy feeling present. I decide to join Col and Tim on the little wooden boat that we had towed behind. We are rowed over to the island. The boys snorkel while I walk along the edge of the beach collecting shells and driftwood. I feel much better walking around and have collected a small bag of interesting bits and pieces. We row back to the boat and climb aboard. Col has forgotten his dive vest at home and has heard there are a lot of jellyfish around so he covers his head with a large crepe bandage. He looks like someone out of the revenge of the Sea Mummy. The trip back is less adventurous and we even manage to wolf down the tuna salad rolls I'd brought with us.

This morning Lindy tells me that her friend Louise had gone out last night and come in after 6am looking the worse for wear.

"She and her boyfriend were stopped by the traffic police, with the works; flashing lights, siren going and radios blaring." Recounts Lindy switching on her computer.

"They were asked to get out of the car which her friend Alan from Al-Hussan compound was driving." She and Alan have been seeing each other the last few weeks and having a ball. Louise said she'd felt so terrified that she'd wanted to puke but felt that this would have revealed all the evidence of her alcohol consumption. Apparently one of the officers had asked Alan if he'd been drinking to which he'd replied,

"I'm sorry I don't understand Arabic." which would have been fine except that he'd been speaking English! In any event they were allowed to go. Extremely lucky I think. They could have been deported for drinking, driving under the influence as well as not being married to each other, several severe offences in Arabia.

Today is a really busy day again. Eight new staff members for in-service arrive at the same time as the man from maintenance to draw up my cupboards from the plan I'd made. The video I leave with the in-service group isn't only the wrong one (choking!) it is in Arabic. So I have to keep jumping in and improvising, dashing out and seeing to cupboards, answer some queries from Dr. Mansour and give Ding some papers for photocopying. Then I present a lecture to Lindy's first group of ICU course nurses. Dr. H keeps coming in and doing his, '*hihowareyouallthebest*' routine, which he does when he's bored.

Lindy and I club together to buy Dr. Al-Hammad a camel tie for his birthday. He's very pleased with it and wears it almost everyday this week before leaving for Japan. He has a quick chat with himself in the cupboard reflection before he leaves which makes me giggle and I have to turn it into a cough.

"You girls must continue with your hard work.," he says opening the fridge and extracting the ever present juice cans. We nod sincerely but have no intentions of overdoing it. No one else does and we are learning that our energy is best conserved for dealing with matters of Saudi bureaucracy.

I take the taxi in to work most days now, sitting behind some well-oiled head, the interior inevitably smelling like a perfume factory. There is always a box of tissues and some other seat covering. One driver has lurid purple towels draped over his seats. Another has fake plastic grass sprouting all over the back seat. It is often a strange strained affair that usually takes place in complete silence. Foreign taxi drivers are there mainly to ferry the western women around. It is haram for the local women to travel alone in a car without their male family member present.

As we arrive outside the main gate of Airbase the driver has to climb out with my gate pass and his *aqama*. After a minute or five, depending on the length of the queue, he will jump back in the taxi and drive a kilometre or so further to the second gate where the procedure is repeated. I am at last deposited outside the education building front gate where I then have to wait for Astor, Ding or Victor to open up. It's like Fort Knox.

I hear today about a huge unfinished building outside town. Apparently they had almost completed the building when someone noticed the different coloured bricks had formed an inadvertent cross design alongside one wall. The decision is made to stop all work and leave the building as it is until they can figure out what to do about the shape of the bricks. This would explain why they have a *Red Crescent* society here instead of Red Cross.

Later this afternoon after lecturing for most of the morning, Lindy files her nails and I read to her some cocktail recipes that big Sue has left us. We are still laughing as we walk to the security office to collect our hospital ID badges. We've done without them for two and half months but we decide we aren't doing much at the moment, (another fit of giggles!) so off we troop.

When we get there they say they can't find Lindy's photo so she scrabbles through piles of application papers to see if she can find it for them.

"Maybe it is attached to the wrong form." She doesn't find it and is sent back to the office for another photo. I decide to wait for her and look across the room to see two Arab security officials sitting next to each other. One is gazing deeply into the eyes of the older Arab. He holds the older man's hand in his, stroking it gently. Next minute as I watch in amazement, the older man whips his arm away and brings it down in mock ferocity over the younger man's arm, chopping away as though his life depended on it. I turn quickly to the security officer looking for my ID to see if he has noticed but instead of Abdullah, Faizel is sitting there looking at me nonchalantly. I look back at the two Arabs and they are now hugging each other fondly. I decide I am in wonderland.

Lindy returns with her photo but now it seems she is short of an *aqama* so off she trots again with one of her broken shoes flapping like a dry tongue. Her new shoes had been a bad buy! I sit and wait for her return having been given my hospital ID badge and signed ten different forms to this effect. She returns with her *aqama* and eventually she is given an ID badge. I leave her wrapping an elastic band around her broken shoe and shuffle off to the policy meeting, which continues in similar vein with all of us making strange suggestions. We speculate whether alcohol swabs would be considered a *no-no* here due to its high alcohol content. Sue says she'd like to dip a couple in some gin and see if it tastes like a G and

T! We all cackle with mirth and I fear the demise of the policy committee sooner rather than later.

Back in the office I note that Lindy now has two elastic bands over her broken shoe. We marvel at how we've both changed. A month ago wearing such shoes to work would have been unthinkable.

I've misplaced my policy notes. Lindy phones the cafeteria to see if I've left them there and the ensuing conversation with the elderly Filipino waitress leaves us in stitches again.

Lindy: "Hello, is that the cafeteria?"

Waitress: "Hello, this is *capeteeriah*"

Lindy: "This is Lindy from Education. Have you seen Janette's notes?"

Waitress: "Hello, who is this?"

Lindy: "It's Lindy from Education, we are looking for papers for Janette. Did she leave it there?"

Waitress: "We *hab botato bie* and *graybee or cheekin* curry."

Lindy: "Oh all right, give us two *botato bies.*"

Waitress: "We are closed. Please *pone* later *aftah* half past *por.*"

Col leaves for Egypt today and it's quiet on the home front.

I have to see Dr. Faziem for my cold and he books me off for the rest of the afternoon. He is looking smug because he has for once a good reason to listen to my chest! Despite feeling really grotty I take Tim into town this afternoon cause he's bored! We pile into the *married* bus, which inexplicably drops us outside gate Two, and there we wait for half an hour for another bus to take us into town. Eventually a large Arab driver arrives and climbs on board in an unhurried fashion. We set off and it soon becomes apparent that we have the driver from hell on board. He isn't interested in keeping his eyes on the road and instead combs his beard, picks his teeth and then looks under his seat for something while driving with his knees! We have one or two near misses and I'm clutching the seat in front praying we get there in one piece.

Later at home I have to wait for the satellite specialist to arrive and sort out the problem we're having. The problem is simple; we don't have a picture and no sound. In effect we don't have satellite. The specialist walks in on a wave of *Brute for men* and starts climbing all over the roof looking for our satellite to move around. It was a while before I realize he's been fiddling with John and Nicki's satellite. I point out the right one and he sets off again. At last he's finished and so am I. My headache and cold have made me deaf and thickheaded. My nose is red and dripping. It is at this point that the satellite chap asks for some orange juice. Then he asks for the bathroom. He returns, sits down and asks me if I like dancing. I don't know where this is going and I don't want to. I tell him I like sleeping but this just steers him in a direction I definitely don't want to go. When he asks to see the bedroom I'm up in a flash and steer him to the door telling him to be off the premises or I'll call security. He's down the steps with an alacrity that was sorely missing in the hour he's been here and I fall into bed exhausted.

I feel terrible the next morning. Lindy insists I stay at home and rest. She says she'll let Dr. H know. I see Tim off on the school bus and fall back into bed. The phone rings twenty minutes later. Lindy says I have to go into work to be booked off!

"What! But that's forty minutes away." I wail. Lindy agrees but says they are adamant. I phone Faziem and ask him to extend my sick leave but he says he can't.

"It's not my rule." he says, I can almost see his raised hands in supplication. I tell him what I think of his rules and slam the phone down. Doctor Farieda, our South African neighbor agrees to write me a sick note, bless her. I spend the rest of the day in bed until Tim comes home from school.

Col is back from his dive weekend. We catch up and have an early night.

Lindy and I leave work after the 'weekend' in-service. We meet Louise and walk into a very quiet town centre. I'd forgotten everything closes between 1pm and 4pm for *siesta* or whatever the Saudi equivalent is. Everything is so strange and still when shut up and closed for the afternoon and it shows a rather grubby exterior, which is missed when everyone's milling around and the shutters are open displaying their wares.

I am constantly amazed at the extent to which the Muttawan go to ensure no wares on display show any sign of female flesh. In the toy section of one department store an inflatable paddling pool sports a family of four frolicking in said pool. The mother appears to be wearing an *abaya* courtesy of the Muttawan heavy hand with the felt tip pen. The other advertises a toddler in a bright yellow swimming tube held aloft by a disembodied head and some sinister black smoke!

They don't advertise in Saudi so everything is word of mouth. For this reason I can't find any telephone numbers for any services when I need them.

We visit a British compound tonight for a rugby match. South Africa plays against UK. The match is going to be shown at Brian's' bar. He has settees and chairs set up facing a large screen. Loads of weak homemade beer on tap served by Brian himself. Len is there leering at Lindy. We sit in groups of two and three. The game keeps the two sides cheering as the room is almost equally divided between SA and the Brits. I'm not always sure who I am cheering for seeing as I'm mostly Brit myself but in any event SA wins 44-23 and I cheer along with enthusiasm with the rest of my SA colleagues.

We finish quite a few packets of crisps and drink quite a few home brews so everyone is feeling both full and merry in equal measure.

Col is hopping up and down outside wáiting to take me home. We stop on the way for a Baskin Robbins ice cream. I am still wearing my jeans and t-shirt and it's nice for once not to have an *abaya* billowing behind me.

We watch a bit of Tim's video this evening, taken for the harvest time festival where he played a sheaf of wheat his school play.

Today is international day at the school. I have to dress Tim up in South African national dress. I figure the Zulu dress wouldn't do as well as a typical Boer. I hunt around for a pair of 'short' shorts, socks, shoes and a comb to put in the socks. Col's bush hat completes the metamorphosis. I also have to draw and paint a South African flag. Have a little trouble with remembering where the actual colours go on the '*Y-fronts.*' Next I have to produce a typical South African recipe. We don't have anything resembling *boerewors, koeksisters or bredie* so I settle for an attempt at *meltert* (milk tart) using crushed biscuits and an instant vanilla whip for the custard.

* * *

Meltert
Ingredients:
1 pack tennis Biscuits
1 tin Condensed Milk
3 cups of warm water
15ml Margarine
100ml Maizena

75ml cold water
1ts vanilla essence
2 medium eggs

Instructions:

Arrange the tennis biscuits in a dish, making a base for the mixture.

Mix the condensed milk, margarine, warm water and microwave for 3 minutes on high. Mix the maizena flour, cold water, vanilla essence and eggs in a separate bowl. Combine the two mixtures. Microwave for 5 minutes on high. Hand Whisk the mixture until the consistency is smooth (not too long) then slowly pour the mixture over the tennis biscuits. Sprinkle cinnamon to taste.

Set in the Fridge.

Tim leaves for school waving his flag, which has wilted a bit as the straw I have used for the handle has bent.

This evening Col and I settle down to watch a bit of telly. We debate whether to have red or white wine. To ease the decision process somewhat we decide to have both! I am pleased with my red. I made it a few weeks earlier using a tried and tested recipe given me by Big Sue. Winemaking, Saudi style, involves mixing a couple of litres of red grape juice (SA variety is best) with sugar, yeast and tea. The intricate fermentation process involves the use of a twenty-litre water container, rinsed well and a chest drain. The latter I manage to get from the surgical ward without raising an eyebrow by saying I am going to give a lecture on chest drains although I did detect a slightly cynically raised eyebrow from Cathy as I saunter by with it. Naturally, the wine has to be kept well hidden as its presence would spell the instant termination of our contracts.

Having been locked out of our offices for the umpteenth time again this morning, Lindy and I decide to take an early bus to the Corniche centre. En route she asks the driver to stop near a shopping mall. I mentioned earlier to Lindy, that I needed to buy some jeans. I scuttle behind her as she strolls with ease over four lanes of traffic with cars screeching to a halt within centimetres of us. I am petrified but Lindy assures me they *will* stop in time.

The SMAA store is still closed for prayers but Lindy convinces them to let us in. They sell a variety of clothes and soon I have a bundle of tops in my arms. Louise has joined us and also found a pile of possibilities. We ask the assistant where we can try on the clothes. He shakes his head,

"No possible," he adds, "you can take clothes to try at home and bring back later". This seems reasonable if a little too trusting to me but Louise argues that she doesn't want to have to return.

She asks again if there is a room to change into and try on the clothes. He again says no. Louise starts to strip off in the aisle; she gets no further than her *abaya* when she gets the key to the ladies thrust hastily into her hand.

In five minutes we are all three changing in the somewhat cramped confines of the ladies toilet.

I also buy a pair of jeans without trying them on and two tea strainers and we walk back along the *corniche* towards the Nurse's centre. The air is a relatively cool 38° C and there are strips of green around us in the well-maintained verges. A coolish breeze allows the sweat to dry. The uniforms we have on are not for walking around in high temperatures. Having found a quaint little coffee shop we sink gratefully into the soft leather chairs within the confines of the *family* section. The décor is dark with a lot of pseudo leopard and zebra print. We each order a different flavour of cheesecake: mousse, apple and strudel. I leave the other two at the centre and take a taxi back to hospital where Col and Tim are waiting for their supper.

Lindy and I meet Leanne briefly then try to provide our respective lectures to the staff. No-one turns up to mine and Lindy cancels hers as the overhead equipment isn't working. I take my monthly report to Dr H. but he isn't there. The computer isn't working. So we give up and take the executive limo into town. They drop us off at a local hotel for tea during prayer time. Lindy and I are led into a small room with awful décor. Plastic chairs and plants trail in rigid abandon around the room, fake white flower stalagtites threaten to topple onto us. The Indian waiter brings us a menu and turns on the nearby water feature. The splash and gurgle of water reminds me I have full bladder. We are told that we can have coffee or juice, as it is prayer time. We order coffee and ask for water in the meantime. For some reason he returns ten minutes later bearing a tray with two tall glasses of black tea complete with tea bag. No sign of the coffee we'd originally ordered or any sugar or milk. Lindy and I valiantly sip on the awful bitter brew but find we can't finish it. We have to pay SR5 for the privilege and we vow never to enter their doorway again, not before nipping quickly into the Ladies though.

As we turn the corner towards Tammimi's store we are almost knocked off our feet by a car that is turning at around 90km an hour. He swerves at the last minute and skids to a halt further up the road. Lindy and I are white and shaken and decide to turn the other way before he comes after us. We eventually enter the cool interior of Tammimi still wobbly kneed. We decide the best way to get over our near miss is by sampling all the freebies on offer. They usually have plates filled with bite-sized samples of their wares dotted around the store and we set to sampling everything on offer with gusto. There are pieces of spicy sausage and cubes of cheese, nestled against pickles and olives. Mini bites of cheesecake sit alongside bite-sized pastries oozing with honey. Sweetmeats nestle alongside small chocolates. We finish off with a small bowl of pancit (a typical Filipino meal consisting long thin strands of noodles with chicken strips and stir fried vegetables). Pancit was introduced to the Philippines by the Chinese and is now a popular part of their cuisine.

"Very tasty." I burp my appreciation and lick the tasty sauce off my fingers. We look at each other and laugh. What a life.

We get a lift back with Robert the hospital engineer.

His wife has just been tested positive with Hepatitis C so luckily for us the ensuing discussion as to her treatment distracts him from asking what we are doing in town during work hours.

Col drives to the local garage later to try and get a slow leak in one of the Toyota wheels fixed. Just as they have the car up on blocks I am wondering how much time we have until prayer time. My question is answered as within five minutes the muezzin call to prayer rings hauntingly over the still hot afternoon air. Immediately all work stops. The garage attendants disappear into the attached mosque to wash and pray and we are left standing around in the heat. I am wearing a short-sleeved dress of a thin cotton material and never have I felt so exposed! Amazing really how the country's imposed beliefs infiltrate the psyche until you feel as I do now, as though I am standing naked in this strictest of Moslem countries, guilty of a huge offence. I pace up and down with my arms wrapped around my middle and try and keep as far as I can from the doorway of the mosque.

Eventually they appear and fix the tyres. I can safely jump back into the land cruiser.

We set off for Al-Jazar compound to meet some friends, Rob and Bev who hail from Joburg, in South Africa. They have invited us for a braai (BBQ). It is Halloween and everyone under twelve years of age is wandering around in a costume. Black and orange colours dominate. Tim is crestfallen to hear we are too late for '*trickle treating*'—trick or treating. The girls intervene and soon Tim is dressed up as a witch complete with pointed hat (he's too young, luckily to realize he is the wrong sex for this costume!) They disappear for half an hour and return with a basket full of goodies. Tim is grinning from ear to ear.

Bev shows me around their apartment. It is smaller than ours but lies on ground floor so they have a small BBQ area around the side of the apartment. The rooms are tastefully furnished in beige and cream with red Arabian cushions and tapestries for colour. We have a good time and enjoy a great braai with fresh salad and bread all washed down with the ubiquitous home brew.

Lindy and I are locked out of the office again. We sit on the steps and chat until Rehaad ambles in at 8:20. He just couldn't care less. Lucky for him Dr. H is away.

Later this afternoon, on the bus to the Corniche centre, we hear from Maria that there is a big *mushkula* (problem) today regarding one of the patients in female medical. The story goes that her nephew visited a Saudi woman in the ward last week. The watchers and nurses of the ward had 'witnessed' some goings on between the nephew and one of the Indian watchers by crawling on their stomachs and looking under the bed screen. They reported '*suspicious*' movements between the nephew and watcher while his elderly sick mother slept. The other watchers report this to the security and not long afterwards the Indian watcher is dragged off and locked up. Her fate is sealed. It doesn't matter that the nephew had forced himself on the poor girl. She is guilty for being in the country and thereby *enticing* him with her feminine charms! They have to now decide whether the event took place from the front (which would result in a beheading) or from behind (which means she'll get a hundred lashes). How horrible for the poor girl. I'm just digesting this story when the bus suddenly runs over a mattress that is lying in the road and we are momentarily jerked out of our seats.

Later this evening we visit the British compound and end up at Brian's pool. We have a BBQ and rolls for supper and watch the game between Australia and South Africa. The *Ossie's* win and Lindy et al are upset. We finish the evening with a darts game. Tim and I play against Amelia and Colin. Tim manages to score a bull's-eye. He is very pleased with himself.

To celebrate Tim has a variety show later for Col and I who desperately try to stay awake and not yawn during his performance of karaoke and a (thankfully) short piano concerto on his small electric piano. He's been on his own all day. He's fighting again with Kurien and Joseph so we have to humour him. As I tidy up afterwards I vow to get them together again by any means. Tim has threatened another 'show' again tomorrow!

I attend the medical education meeting in lieu of Dr. Al-Hammad. It is as boring as all hell. The doctors can't come to any decision on anything, preferring rather, to painfully pontificate every point. They spend twenty-five minutes trying to pass a document that's been on the agenda for two years! Ditto the case of the missing journals. Apparently a set of medical journals was purchased a few years ago, which subsequently went missing. This has been discussed *ad nauseum* at every meeting since. I present my report on educational activities and try to throw in my own point of view every now and then but get no response. I am woman. I menstruate therefore anything I say is automatically suspect. This is unfortunately a common feeling between Saudi's and other similar nationals.

Leanne phones me this afternoon and asks me when my next orientation for this month will be. I suppress a giggle because I haven't even done the first one yet but manage to give her a date.

We have a Guy Fawkes bonfire at this weeks hash. I have spent a few hours making my 'guy'. The best one wins a prize. I have *borrowed* one of the spare CPR doll's faces from work and figure this has got to make him the most lifelike! We get a lift with Len in his office car.

Others run the hash but Tim, Lindy, Delia and I amble along chatting. We see nothing but an old goat and a couple of fossilized camel bones.

The judging takes place and I get first prize theoretically but 2nd prize in practice which is fine because it's really for the kids and the prize is a Mickey Mouse pen and watch set which I didn't really want. Honest!

I am angry this morning because we are locked out yet again and I have an orientation programme to run. When the door is eventually opened I try and sort out the venue. Get all the new staff into the auditorium and start with lectures. Suddenly the door opens and one of the Filipino nurses tells me that we must whisper as we are on the same corridor as Prince Banda who is complaining of the noise. I try and whisper the lecture on infection control but eventually give up feeling ridiculous. I leave Mama Huud screeching her lecture on Saudi culture. Let *her* try and explain that to the prince!

I am so tired by the time my limo comes that I hop in front with the driver. I quickly I realize my mistake and hop out again. The driver smiles, nods his head sideways and says *mufee mushkila,* but I know better!

I try and get my exit entry visa renewed so I can go on leave in December. Nothing doing. I'm worried because I can't leave the country without it. Col has already got his and Tim's sorted out. Darn country. They make it so difficult to do anything normally I think irritably.

We rush around town later trying to sort out the plane tickets to Sweden. The travel man managed to stuff up the ticket dates. Then we rush over to Giant stores to do the shopping. I buy enough for a month. It's no fun shopping anymore. You just try and rush between prayers and bad driving. I buy Tim a small dartboard and tonight he goes to sleep clutching teddy, panda, his new toy car and the dartboard.

I collect my exit visa today from captain *Ahmed Moosa God* I thought that was taking religion a bit too far but, who am I? As my dear departed gran would say!

We have supper with John and Nicci. I marvel at their apartment so alike ours in design yet so beautifully furnished. No sign of the horrid brown and orange colours that we have. Their colour scheme is beige and russet. There are beautifully coloured glass hubbly-bubblies and lacquered cabinets, silver ornaments, wooden boats and rich red carpets.

The table has been beautifully set with silver platters and crystal Czechoslovakian wine glasses.

A tall man with dark hair and pale chiseled features joins us for dinner. He offers me a limp handshake and says his name is Serge.

I give Nicci a bottle of my best home brew. She opens the cap and takes a sniff.

"Hmm, it's lovely. I'll put it away for another month." Obviously smells awful! Everyone enjoys my homemade *Baileys whisky cream* though, which makes me feel better. Another couple join us as we are about to eat. They are both Polish and work with John. The conversation is peppered with Saudi flavoured anecdotes and there is much laughter.

We hear that it used to be very nice living at this compound with *wild parties and many more Westerners than now.*

Serge tells us about a Saudi pilot coming in to land with his cell phone glued to his ear under his helmet. The cell phone naturally interferes with the electronics and the readings go haywire. With the resultant decompression both cell phone and helmet expand so that it becomes impossible to remove and increasingly more painful. The pilot is talked down by ground control and he has to have the cell phone surgically removed. I wondered how this could happen but decide anything is possible in the land of lost logic!

CHAPTER NINE

"Travel is glamorous only in retrospect."

Paul Theroux

American Compound

THE NEXT MORNING, I find myself waiting, yet again, for the taxi. They are twenty minutes late. I phone their office and ask why they aren't here. The Indian man tells me their phones aren't working. When I ask him how is it possible that we are now able to converse on his phone there is a silence and the phone goes dead. Just as I'm picturing boiling the whole bloody lot in hot oil they phone back. I am nearly in tears with frustration. I have a room full of orientees waiting for me at the hospital. I curse the country and the law that prevents women from driving. I phone Lindy and ask her to please see to the orientees till I get there. The taxi arrives at 9:20. It is a new driver and I have to explain to him how to get to the hospital. We drive at a snails pace due to two separate car accidents along the way. It is not going to be my day. This proves true when we get to the main gate and the security decide they haven't seen me nearly every day for the past six months and demand my ID.

In my haste I present my home compound gate pass. The security guard hands it back and refuses to let me in till I retrieve the correct pass from the depths of my handbag, which takes ages as I'm flustered and seething with irritation by now. After flinging my bag into the office, I run down to the auditorium and take over from Lindy who is discussing pork recipes with them.

I quickly take over before we are in trouble but am not really prepared and ad-lib my way through the rest of the awful morning.

By now I have a terrible headache and sit with my head in my hands when Victor pops his *brylcreamed* head round the door and asks what's wrong.

He brings me a plate of cold spaghetti to cheer me up, which is very kind but I have to discreetly chuck in to the waste bin as soon as his shiny dark head has disappeared.

We meet at Sharon and Phil's later on for supper. I help make the salads. Trevor, Lindy and an Irish bloke called Martin is also there. I also meet Tony. He's quite precious and definitely has more than five fingers on each hand. Turns out he was the last English language instructor at the hospital. Before Glen, our present instructor was hired. We have still to meet him though. He talks disparagingly about Dr. Al-Hammad and Mr. Aziz. He left under a bit of a cloud I gather. Tony regales another story from the *green truth*. Seems someone has written in to ask the resident imam what to do about his fetish. Turns out he keeps his wife pregnant, as he's quite partial to breast milk! He apparently asks if the Koran is OK with this and the serious answer is, *yup, it's OK to suckle* at wife's boob as long as he didn't partake of a full meal and thereby deprive little Mohammed of his supper. Gross!

We meet up with Trevor and he fills us in with the nights events after we left last night. Apparently Sharon got into a steamy clinch with some chap and was dragged off by Phil and given a belting. That's why I like to leave early!

I have to take an earlier taxi back to our compound after work to collect Jenny and Lindy who are attending a course there. I get some young Saudi driver who decides he is at *kyalami*. His average speed is 160 km an hour. My hands do leave the roof and my bottom never touches the seat! I totter out of the cab and ask the driver to wait for Lindy and Jenny to take them back to the hospital. He doesn't understand a word I am saying so I flag down another Saudi passerby and ask if he will explain to him but he can't understand either. I scout around and eventually find a blond haired nurse. Surely she speaks English! She does but with a strong European accent but, and this is the best part, she can speak Arabic! Problem solved. Her name is Zolla and she's from Iceland. The taxi driver waits for the other two and I thank her and go to find Tim who had been home alone all day with a bad cold.

The limo arrives late again so Lindy and I take the back entrance of the hospital. This gate has plastic palm trees and mock castle turret type gates but nothing for five km between there and the hospital but sand and old machinery. We sneak in and I am just in time to answer a call from Rehaad. He just wants to find out if I am there. The snake, I think a little unreasonably.

I have a review group lecture this morning. I can't believe how they do things here. For IV therapy the bag, needle and tube are all labeled with little sticky post-it's that read, 'bag', 'tube' and 'needle'. When asked, they inform me that this is to remind them to change the tubing etc. I ask them if they'd label the patient's clothing to make sure they changed them too but my sarcasm gets no response.

We are chatting outside the hospital and see the limo take off. I wonder why Lindy is running after it and then remember I'm supposed to be in it! This trip is as bad as the other day if not worse. The car doesn't have a speedometer but I estimate from the total blur outside my window that we are going very fast. This will explain why we manage to make the normally twenty-five minute journey in fourteen minutes!

The return journey doesn't improve. Lindy phones me at 3:15 to say they are ready to be collected. I trot down to transport and get a limo. Just as we leave the main gate, Saiid discovers we have no petrol. He drives back in and I think we'll change vehicles or something but no, he just collects a piece of paper that allows him to buy petrol. I see him turn towards town and begin to protest. He shrugs and says he must fill up at a pre-designated petrol station in the centre of town. Well actually he says, "I go petrol Khyber." which means the same thing really. I sit in the back fuming. I imagine Lindy and Jenny are wondering what has happened to us and there's no way of communicating. I am astounded to see he keeps the engine running while filling up. I am just thinking at least he's not smoking when he fumbles for a cigarette from his voluminous trouser pocket under his *Thobe*. "No, No!" I exclaim. He turns towards me, cigarette dangling from his lip, *"muffee smoke!"* I say again mimicking the throwing away of cigarettes. Thankfully he understands and complies. He also gets the fact that I'm anxious that we'll be late and obliges by driving extremely fast towards KWMH. When we get there, there is no sign of either Lindy or Jenny. I wait a further ten hot minutes then tell him to leave. Lindy phones later and says they had already left at 4pm. I wisely hold my tongue.

Lindy's ICU course starts this morning but it hasn't gone well at all so far. Firstly we are locked out again till well after 8am. Then Lindy hears that her two students who come from KWMH, our resident hospital have been refused entry to this one. Their gate passes are removed. This is a big problem as one of them is mine! I'd given it to Lindy to make it easier for her student to attend the course. She gave the other student her own gate pass. Luckily it is all sorted out with a brief explanation from Rehaad and I leave unscathed at 1pm, reunited with my gate pass.

Col, Tim and I have a walk in the desert again. We are desperate to find some wildlife and trudge over the rolling dunes in search of something interesting. Unfortunately all we see in two hours is a dung beetle and a sand tit.

The sun sinks over the dunes in a red haze and we start the long walk back towards the car. We are walking in the moonlight to where we thought we'd parked the car only it isn't there! Tim and I sit down to lean against a soft dune while Col, walks further on to see if he can find it. He returns ten minutes later. "It was at the next dune," he explains climbing into the driver's seat.

As we drive back to the hospital another huge 4X4 almost drives into us, headlights are blazing, horn tooting. Col instinctively turns to the left and we miss each other by centimetres. Shaken we continue on a little further before noticing a car behind us. It is the same car. They pull up close to us and an angry bearded face appears through the open window. It transpires we had been driving on the wrong side of the road earlier! Luckily Col is able to calm them down as it could have been quite ugly. We are out in the desert with no-one but the moon. He explains and points to Tim and me. I give my brightest smile and shrug as though to say, "we all make mistakes, sorry". They don't look too happy but thankfully turn and drive back the way they had come and we heave a collective sigh of relief.

We arrive at Tim's school at the appointed hour. Today is Mohammed's birthday (the school mate not the prophet!) and we are to meet Mohammed's mother, Fawzia Al-Somali and the other guests for his birthday party, which is to be held inside the American compound on their private beach.

Fawzia arrives late and emerges from their limo, a tall graceful woman in a flurry of apologies and flowing headgear. Her *abaya* is a beautiful floating silk affair that billows extravagantly behind her as she rushes forward to meet the rest of the parents and their invited offspring.

"I am so sorry for being late." she says kissing both my cheeks. I catch the whiff of very expensive perfume and a glimpse of her Gucci jeans underneath her *abaya*. Fawzia has small Somali features and long shiny black hair. Her lipsticked smile beams pearly teeth. She is beautiful. Her husband sits behind the wheel of their limo. His role in the proceedings is clear. We barely have time to climb into our respective vehicles and he shoots off in typical Saudi fashion at 150 KM an hour. We all try and keep up and follow him to the compound gates. There is a delay while all the ownership papers and *agama*'s are collected and shown to the security, returned and then we're in. We drive through the manicured lawns of the compound towards their private beach. It is another world. Roads have two lanes and cars drive slowly, stopping at traffic lights.

Gardens are neat and tidy squares of lawn in front of typically American clapboard houses. Women walk around in shorts and T-shirts. Children run up and down on bicycles or roller blades. Manicured women sway along the street. Trails of flowers run over verandahs. We have landed in Wisteria Lane in a scene from Desperate Housewives! Soon we are in front of another set of white washed gates. Fawzia hands the security some more papers and presumably pays for us and soon we are inside. The beach is picture postcard. Green rolling lawns, tall palms, white sand and a turquoise sea.

Only the Americans could organize this oasis in the middle of the desert I think looking around in wonder. The day is hot but pleasant with a cool offshore breeze. We all group together on the beach and chat generally while the soft breeze lifts our hair and caresses our cheeks. The Al-Somalis prepare for the party. There is one other Saudi couple and she is veiled from top to toe. Other than her the rest of the party are westerners like ourselves. One other woman wears thick black stockings and a headscarf loosely around her head. The Saudi men traditionally sit apart from the women and I see some of the other dads looking from this group to ours, a little unsure of protocol. The children swim in the warm gulf water and we sit around chatting to each other. Fawzia flits from one group to another smiling and chatting, the eternal host. At midday she calls us all inside the long building which serves as the restaurant. We are given burgers and juice for lunch. As I sit down with Col and some other parents I notice that the restaurant has both a traditional and western dress code. Abaya and thobe sit side by side with shorts and T-shirts. I almost feel embarrassed for the Americans flouting of custom.

I hear that the Saudi part of the compound is growing steadily and Saudi-ization is slowly infiltrating the traditional American way of life.

After our meal we go for a walk on the beach. Again I notice small groups of veiled and fully covered women sitting with men in *ghutra and thobe*. They smoke hubbly bubblys and seem unperturbed by the scantily dressed westerners who walk by in their bikinis and swimming costumes. Teenage Saudi's look covertly at some other lesser dressed teens and I wonder what they make of this. I walk along picking up shells and driftwood chatting to Col about our future. We have to stay at least a couple of years in order to be able to go home and buy a bigger house we decide.

Tim is trying to fly a bright red and blue kite and his little face is lit up with excitement. Fawzia comes to us and puts her slim arm around my ample middle.

"I hope you have enjoyed the day.," she asks smiling her pearly whites.

We both nod in agreement. "You must just phone me if you want to come anytime again." she says and drifts off to say goodbye to some other parents.

It has been an interesting day but we are all tired so we also leave soon after. We see a large sign at one of the petrol stations on the way home proclaiming it to have *laundry for car.*

Work passes in a busy routine with me doing *recerts* and Lindy finishing her course. We meet up with Delia after work and go for some supper.

There are a variety of curries to choose from. Afterwards we walk for miles chatting about this and that. The pavements are cracked and uneven. The doorways of shops are brightly lit against the dark. Strategically placed buckets collect the drips from leaky air conditioners. I see many shops have *festive* cards on display it being close to Christmas. This is strange given the feelings about anything Christian. I see they are careful to say *happy holidays* or merry *festivities* and avoid any mention of the jolly old chap in red. One card has a huge drawing of a piece of holly, but the figure is that of a chewing camel not father Christmas. There are even Christmas lights (called *festive decorations* on the label!) I notice with amusement.

This evening Col, Tim and I drive into town for another birthday party at McDonalds for a schoolmate of Tim's. We stop en route to buy a gift at the 20 Riyal store. I am still wrapping it up as we arrive virtually the first ones there. A birthday section has been cordoned off upstairs. We greet the parents (mother is dressed in *abaya* and veil). The birthday cake has both Abdul and his younger brother's name decorated on it in lurid icing so as not to make him feel left out. Col and I want to pop into the bookstore before prayer time so we leave Tim there and say we'll be back shortly. We wander around Al-Jarirs looking at books and CDs for sale. As the first wail of prayer rents the air we leave and take a walk along the *corniche*. It is a beautiful evening. The moon is large and bright. The recently waning sun has set on a pastel sea. The water's edge is tinted gold and mauve with a silver veil of mist coming in from the sea. We see flying fish skimming over the flat water.

Reluctantly we return to the plastic world of McDonalds and their equally plastic burgers.

By this time the party is in full swing with loud music, crowds and screaming children. It is strange to see the western parents sitting in the familiar plastic seated chairs while in another room, off the main one, a large number of Saudi women; all veiled, are chatting and eating. The tables are now groaning with every local delicacy you can imagine. I open the door and look around uncertainly.

"Help yourself." smiles a small woman in a dark embroidered *abaya*. Her face veil is lifted revealing cracked yellowing teeth. I pick up a plate and under the watchful gaze of another large Egyptian woman I lift some samosas onto it with my left hand. I realize my mistake the minute the frown cross her large features. I hastily swop hands and burble quickly about the lovely food and say the cook must be congratulated. I redeem myself. She *is* the cook and she tells me how she wraps the vine leaves around glutinous rice to make the long greenish pieces I have picked up.

No-one is especially friendly though so I leave the room to fetch Colin. I tell him to go and help himself, which he does. It is while I'm pushing the last morsel of sticky rice into my mouth that I realise my mistake. I rush over to the door and look inside. Col is standing next to one of the tables slowly piling his plate high with goodies while behind him all hell is breaking loose as women hastily fling their veils over their faces. Some women are trying to find their *niqāb's* (face covering) and hastily tie them behind their heads, others are stuffing their food and veils into their mouths at the same time in their haste to cover up before he turns round. One woman shoves a huge egg roll under her veiled chin and turns round presumably to swallow the thing whole. I sidle up to Col and hiss at him to stop and come outside. He looks around and sees a row of covered women staring (one imagines) at him. Col gives a half wave and leaves the room with his plate of delicacies.

"What happened in there?" he asks popping a humus and tomato crisp into his mouth.

"Cat among the pigeons." I reply somewhat enigmatically.

Second prayer comes as we are finishing off our meal and we suddenly find ourselves sitting in the dark feeling the table for napkins and cold coffee. The gloom does wonders for a birthday atmosphere!

It is Friday morning. We are rushing around trying to get ready for a day in the mountainous area of Hofuf, which is located around the metropolitan area of Dhahran, Al-Khobar and Dammam, a few hundred Km's away. Hofuf means whistling wind in Arabic and is one of the major cultural centers in Saudi Arabia. We meet up with Anthony Carson. He is English and the desert naturalist as well the math's and science teacher for the local university. Thin and wiry with a neat moustache and glasses, Anthony meets us outside *dune 4* with some others. We drive our 4X4's over the desert. We have let some air out from the tyres to make it easier to drive, as it's difficult gripping the sand. Col is managing this difficult task with aplomb but concentration is a must. We drive to an old abandoned fort, one of many in Hofuf, following Anthony and the other two vehicles closely. The fort is made from red mud bricks and is in a poor state of repair. Col walks up the old water tower with Anthony while I look around the rooms, or rather, what's left of them. The roof has long since crumbled away in the heat over the ages. We visit a *sabkhas* (salt pan) and walk across its crusty surface and stop at a sand gully for lunch. It is very hot by now. All we see is a pale coloured lizard. Not much else. We get stuck twice after that in the land cruiser, wheels whirring uselessly under the slippery sand. The others help us out with old blankets. We end the day by traversing the biggest dune I've ever seen. The scary moment poised at the lip of the dune before hurtling down almost vertically. Tim is delighted and wants Col to,

"Do it again daddy."

This steep dune had a 10km dry 'lake' around it. Anthony takes a photo of the three of us standing atop a sloping dune. There are some amazing red sandstone rock carvings in Hofuf. The wind carves unusual shapes into the red strata. We all stop at the garage in Dhahran to pump the tyres up again. Thanking Anthony, we promise to join him again next time.

CHAPTER TEN

"Travel and change of place impart new vigor to the mind."

Seneca

Teatime in the Kingdom

Lᴉɴᴅʏ ᴀɴᴅ I take the 2pm bus to Silver Towers. We hop off at our destination and walk towards the "kingdom of dates." This establishment has every type and description of date sweetmeat imaginable. We spend a pleasant half hour sampling dates with nuts, dates rolled in sesame seeds, date cakes, pistachio and date rolls and even a date ice cream! Thus loaded both in tum and packages we waddle outside towards the chocolate shop. Lindy, having done her 'butt' comes out with chocolate covered dates, nuts, and some shell like chocolate sweets. The swarthy Syrian attendant gives us a free bag of chocolate labels. We make it to a nearby restaurant just as prayer starts. They are just about to close the door when we beg entry saying the heat has got to us (not to mention a few kilos of chocolates and dates!). The mustachioed Indian reluctantly allows us to enter. He motions us upstairs; scared we will be noticed by a passing Muttawa. We climb the stairs and almost stumble over a prostate form at the top. Feeling a little embarrassed, we shuffle past him as he scrambles quickly to his feet to serve us. We have no money to speak of and realize too late this is a restaurant not a coffee shop as we thought at first. We ask for two glasses of water and get a blank look. I grab the menu and point to mango juice. "Bring two." I say holding up my fingers.

Lindy then confuses him further (perhaps he's still wrapped up in religious fervour) and asks for a club soda to go with her mango juice. She tries a variation on the theme, soda water? No comprehension, water with many bubbles brings less of a reaction, as does sparkling water, fizzy water and as a last attempt Lindy takes a spoon and whips it quickly through the air to illustrate a great agitation whilst saying "aqua, aqua." The poor man is backing away from us by now so I smile to show we are really harmless and say, "water".

He returns with two tall glasses. Lindy is given orange juice to which he has apparently added some tonic water. While she takes her first tentative sip, I turn my attention to my glass, which he has set down before me. The colour is an odd yellow green and is so thick and viscous I am convinced he's given me baby food. My straw stands straight up in this thick puréed apple mixture. I bend forward slightly and my trembling lips close around the straw as I attempt to draw the mixture through it. I valiantly 'eat' my drink while Lindy sips her tonic water and orange. Our eyes meet and we begin to laugh. We laugh pretty much until we are presented with the bill.

"What!" I exclaim loudly drawing in a thick mouthful of air and apple purée and coughing wildly for a few seconds,

"SR 25 each for this!" We grumble but pay up. We reason that it *has* helped to while away the time until end of *Asr* (afternoon prayer).

A short word about prayers:

Prayers

Salah or prayer times occur over five periods of the day as part of tradition, which are measured according to the movement of the sun. These are: approaching dawn *(fajr)*, just after midday (dhuhr), in the afternoon (asr), just after sunset *(maghrib)* and at night time *(isha'a)*. Sometimes prayers can be shortened or combined (according to prescribed procedures). Prayers can be skipped when there is a good reason, but they should be made up later. I would have liked to 'skip them' pretty much any time I want to go shopping or somewhere to eat!

We walk quite far along the *corniche* clutching our bags of chocolates and other delicacies purchased along the way. 'Hey, isn't that the place Dr. Hammad was talking about'? Asks Lindy as we trudge up a sidewalk. She's pointing to a coffee shop with black and chrome windows. 'I think so' I peer up at the name, 'Joffrees Coffee shop', it proclaims.

"Let's go in and grab a cup." She peers in through the closed doors and mimes that we'd like to come in to the shadowy figures inside.

The door opens and an Indian man wearing black trousers and a white shirt stands looking mildly annoyed.

"Vee are closed for prayer." he says firmly. But Lindy is not one to give up easily and she persists saying, "We only want a drink and we'll be gone."

We can have take away coffee says the waiter leading us into a small narrow hallway with a long counter against one side. We order a cappuccino for Lindy and a tea for me. There are no chairs so we sink slowly to the steps and Lindy takes out her asthma pump. This brings some action and we suddenly have two plastic seats to sit on.

They are placed just in front of the counter a few steps from the entrance so it looks rather awkward. Lindy's coffee arrives, hot and frothy in a black insulcup, my tea arrives, hot and black. I quickly explain that I take mine white. He whips away the tea in the disposable cup and returns with black tea in a white cup. I shake my head,

'No, I want tea with MILK!' I speak the word slowly more in an effort to control my temper than to allow for understanding. The waiter takes away the cup and returns with tea and what looks like curdled milk. I take a tentative sip and nearly spew it all over the hovering waiter, "MILK," I say again loudly, "but NO LEMON with it!" he removes the cup and walks quickly back to the kitchen. Lindy has almost finished with her coffee and is smiling in amusement. The waiter returns and this time he has two Filipinos in tow. I repeat my order and they exclaim,

"Ah, *por* you, is wanting tea *weeth the meelk but not weeth the leemon*?" I nod and they disappear again.

"Would have been less hassle if they'd just let us sit upstairs and order from a menu" I say to Lindy as she drains her coffee.

I wait expectantly. This time I get a beautifully wrapped disposable cup, insulated with corrugated cardboard! I lift the lid gingerly and peer in. A teabag is suspended above the water by what appears to be a thick brown toothpick. I gently lift the toothpick and a long windsock shaped teabag is revealed. We can contain ourselves no longer, we laugh and laugh till tears come to our eyes. 'Oh what a place' I laugh, wiping my eyes with the back of my hand and sipping on what turns out to be a lovely cuppa. Our hysterical laughter brings a bevy of veiled women from the top of the stairs. They descend and stand looking at us in amazement. Two westerners, in white nurse's uniform, howling with laughter. This of course only sets us off again. The sight of three dark veiled shapes and two bewildered waiters all gazing at us has us gasping for breath. Lindy contains herself long enough to ask the waiter to bring another tea bag for me.

"She want the tea bag?" he asks incredulously pointing at me. I nod and he rushes off and quickly returns with another *windsock* and large brown toothpick carefully wrapped in tissue paper. We explain that we're from South Africa and we want to keep the bag as a memento of our wonderful time in their shop. They nod uncomprehendingly and watch us walk away shaking their heads. This will be something to tell the family when they get home tonight.

We have missed the gulf bus back to the hospital so we go up to Lindy's apartment and freshen up.

We arrive back in time for lock up. Later Rehaad asks me where I've been all afternoon

"Marking CPR test papers." I tell him avoiding eye contact. He grunts but says nothing. I smile to myself. Ah well it was only a couple of hours. It has struck me that this kind of behavior is totally foreign to what I consider my usually responsible nature but months of resistance to my attempts at providing lectures and updating information to the ward nurses has proved useless. As long as I am around the hospital doing something they appear to be satisfied but they do not want any changes to the status quo.

I take a cake to work this morning for Sue's birthday tea in the conference room. Much derision regarding the burnt crust and strange orange icing so I tell Sue that blowing out her candles is going to cause a bonfire!

We receive a notice hand delivered by Rehaad who says we have to read it carefully before signing it. Lindy and I peer at the usual typed photocopy.

It reads:

All hospital staff must display ID prominently for patients and competent (sic) staff, failure will cause retributions (!)

This is all well and good but I have been waiting for my ID for over a month. They say the machine is broken and I must come back again tomorrow, (Ins'Allah!)

We drive to Tim's school to pick up one of the teachers, Deepak. He joined the school recently and wants to dive so Col is going to take him to Jubail.

He has a very English accent so imagine my surprise and delight when he tells me he was brought up in Uganda! He left Kampala when he was nine years old. What a small world. My parents, siblings and I lived in Uganda for twelve years in the sixties. Left because of Idi Amin and his antics, but that's another story.

It is very windy today and the sand is blowing all over the place. Col and Deepak go for a dive. The water, in spite of the wind, is flat and green with only the occasional ripple. Later we have lunch inside the restaurant and being the norm while eating, discussion turns to hand chopping! It seems that when someone has been found guilty of theft, surgeons are doing the dirty deed these days in theatre, to keep things nice and clean by creating a stump! Sound surgical management, for a terrible sentence.

On the way home we have a blow out. The vehicle suddenly swerves into the side of the road. Col handles it very well. It is scary though and so is trying to change the offending tire on the verge with traffic whizzing past us. I'm told to sit in the car when Col realizes that cars are careering dangerously close as I'm not wearing my *abaya,* showing far too much bare skin and my long hair is loose!

We have a new staff member in the Education department. He is Grant Rea from the Philippines, a fresh round-faced man with a ready smile. I help him settle in by showing him around and introducing him to people. His job is to teach the Saudi staff at the hospital including army personnel, how to speak English. This is a daunting task as I have heard most of the staff are not interested in speaking English and feel the lessons to be a waste of time.

Lindy phoned me yesterday to tell me that she has asked Len to buy us some bacon and magazines from Bahrain. He's driving over there this morning. I'm thinking how nice the bacon will be as my taxi swings in to the front of gate one. I notice a sign near the gate that says, *Slow down! Dim lights and prepare for inspection*!

Well if that doesn't put the fear of God (sorry, Allah) into one, I don't know what will!

Lindy brings me my bacon this afternoon, wrapped up in three layers of brown paper. There are two crisp women's magazines for me to read as well. Although the whole will cost me an arm and a leg, it's worth it. Jarirs bookstore does not stock many non-Islamic magazines and I have had nothing worthwhile to read for a while now. I sniff the brown paper but there is no actual smell of pork. Just as well as I've to wander down the hospital corridor with it. Amazing how appreciative one becomes of anything the minute you know it's hard to come by.

It is supposed to be payday today. Lindy gets a cheque but when I go to the ATM in the afternoon there's no money in. I feel angry and helpless. I hate this uncertainty of waiting for a cheque every month. My pay should be deposited into the bank by now but who knows why it isn't—they aren't telling me. So today I arrange for a big bus to take all my new recruits, Delia and myself into town to cash pay cheques and get our money out. We have the typical laconical driver who chews on his toothpick and drives mostly with his knees!

It is also the first day of Ramadan today, which may also account for the general lack of energy!

I try and insert my card at the bank's ATM machine but it is again rejected. Yesterday it worked but today there is a *mushkila*. There is a huge queue inside the bank so I start raving about the useless system. Not a wise thing to do as it only makes everything go slower. When I eventually get to the till I withdraw *all* my money. I figure I'm not going to have a problem every time I want to draw some cash. I'm told that I will have to return for a new card in January.

When we get back I'm accosted by Rehaad who asks where Lindy is. I know exactly were she is but I'm not telling *him* she's driving over the bridge on her way to Bahrain with Len as we speak, so instead I say she's in ICU, "As far as I know." When I get home later I phone her and tell her Rehaad is on the look out. She tells me she bought an ice-cream in town today and was happily licking away at it when a man came up to her yelling, "Ramadan, Ramadan!" Lindy apparently thought he was very happy about it so she paused in her licking and gave him a broad smile, "Happy Ramadan to you too!" He was not amused and when it struck her she may be breaking a few rules by eating in public during this holy month of Ramadan she disappeared quickly down an alleyway before he summonsed the Muttawa! Col is amused when I tell him and declares it the best '*blonde joke*' of the month!

Tonight Delia comes back with Col and me from the hospital. She will look after Tim while we attend the BBB (British Businessman's Ball). The ball is held in Al-Hadisha compound which is next to the dive club. Balloons and other Christmasy stuff are festooned around the compound hall to mark the occasion. I am handed a rose at the door by one of the BBB association staff and clutch it to my chest while entering the hallway to find our table. We are seated with the headmistress of the school and her husband but a real stuffy snotty pair they turn out to be. A Sean Connery lookalike and his wife however are more welcoming. He says they have been in Saudi for nineteen years! Another large balding businessman and his wife complete the table. Although the Sean Connery couple is nice enough we don't really have much in common with the others. The School ma'am and her husband are interested to hear how a 'South African' couple managed to get into the British Businessman's association. We are happy to tell them that both Col and I have British passports (work that out snobs).

Bev and Rob are there and she comes over to chat. We have to buy our own wine, which we think is a bit much given the cost of the tickets (SR 180 each). I walk over to a long table set against a wall and purchase a two litre 'milk bottle' of wine! I remind myself that despite the posh décor we *are* still in Saudi.

Speeches are given including an update on world business affairs. Col and I have a dance; well a shuffle around the dusty floor, which we hope, passes for a dance. We wander over to the bar next door and find Trevor there propped up against the counter. We stay till midnight chatting to him and return to our compound trying not to breathe any alcoholic fumes over the security guards as we wave our gate pass at them, speaking in slow short sentences, enunciating each syllable carefully which, given that speech is usually unnecessary, causes security to stare with suspicion. We enter our apartment with the typically exaggerated walk of the mildly inebriated to find Delia still awake and pounding away on the computer. She says she and Tim had fun.

Despite only a few hours sleep we are up early with headaches, to prepare for a trip to Scribner's canyon, which is just north of Hofuf in Jubail. We meet the others at a nearby dune. Tom, Jean and Chaz, Nicci and John, Gary without Pam, a strange American in a white jumpsuit who continuously encroaches our personal space. Not a good idea when we are both feeling delicate! We set off in convoy about an hour's drive away and park off road near the canyon. I look up in awe at the magnificent reddish pink and yellow sand and limestone rock wind-carved into interesting shapes.

Tom and Anthony are to lead the 'expedition' into the canyon. When everyone arrives Anthony explains that we have to keep close to him as we climb the rocks. We follow him up a dusty sandy pathway to the beginnings of Scribner's. It is quite a walk and at times I find myself having to crawl on my hands and knees through the narrow rock, which leaves a fine layer of pink dust on my clothes. Anthony grabs me up a particularly steep rock where there is hardly any purchase. In one spot I have to climb onto Col's head, which amuses Tim who is finding it all great fun and no effort at all!

At the end of a good hour and a half of intense climbing through narrow paths and up steep rock face, getting bruised and scraped and covered in pigeon shit, we make it to the top of the canyon.

"Wow, look at that!" I gasp out puffs of salmon coloured dust with each word when we are finally able to stand upright and look out over the valley below.

The air is still and hot, the sky an intense blue and this beautiful rock is cut out of the surrounding landscape like a series of ornate carvings. We walk around the top of the canyon for a while then begin our descent, arriving back at base before many of the others. It's tiring but also intensely satisfying. Anthony hands out his famous brownies that he's made especially for the occasion. They are delicious and I reach over and remove another one from the plastic container.

"How old is this place?" I ask between bites of gooey chocolate.

"Two million years ago the desert began to form and the remains of man, his tools and water life such as clams remain around the ancient dried up lakeshore."

Anthony is a mine of information and tells us all about the area. Prehistoric man once inhabited the deserts of Saudi Arabia and they lived around what were once large lakes in the area such as were we are now. After lunch we drive to a small saltpan and look for *desert diamonds,* which are little glass stones that glint in the sun like a jewelry counter. We also look for fossils. We end up with a BBQ in the cool evening desert.

I breathe in the still warm night air and absently stroke one of my fossilized clams.

The door chain at work is firmly in place so I tell the taxi driver to pick me up at 08H00 tomorrow morning. May as well have a fifteen-minute extra sleep in if they're going to continuously keep me from entering the building in the mornings. I phone from the lab to get the door open and find a queue as long as my arm, maybe even longer, waiting for recertification. I'm in the middle of *recerting* about twenty Filipino nurses when Dr. Hammad makes a sudden and dramatic appearance. He's wearing his *thobe* and *ghutra* so I figure he's in one of his fervent moods. He goes into a long and intimate clinch with Dr.*Who* recently returned from Syria then turns his attention to his girls,

"How are you?" he asks gazing fondly at us both. We both say we are well and he beams. "Wonderful." He stands looking at us for some minutes saying,

"Good, good." We beam back at him and wish he'd get a move on. Every time we bump into him for the next few hours he says, "Hallo. *Howareyou*" till we decide to leave the building altogether to avoid saying we're fine for the umpteenth time.

He later tells me in a moment of candour that he found it difficult maintaining Ramadan's strict rules of abstinence while in China. It must be worse for him on home turf so to speak.

Lindy and I get our cheques this morning but as usual there's no money in the bank. "Useless pieces of paper!" I think viciously shoving the crumpled cheque in my uniform pocket. We go shopping anyway seeing as we're in town and I buy some warm clothes and thermal underwear for our upcoming holiday in Sweden. I also buy a Christmas present for Ding, Aster, Glen and Victor. Naturally they will be referred to as *festive gifts.*

I visit the dental department after lunch. My tooth has been hurting again this past week and I'm living on pain tablets. Lyn at dental tries to convince the reluctant dentist that he'd seen me only a couple of weeks ago. He shoves me into the chair and takes out all his frustrations for his poor workmanship on my mouth. He stabs my palette with the needle and I nearly go through the roof it's so painful. With numb mouth and dribbling spittle I visit the cafeteria for lunch. The food for the month of Ramadan is a choice of take-away wrapped in tin foil for the non-Muslims so as not to offend anyone en route to my office. I walk down the corridor with my hot foil package feeling very conspicuous and when I see a Saudi approaching I try and hide it behind my back.

Dr. Hammad is in his office so I pop in later to chat to him and hear more about his trip to China. He says they are very pedantic over there and he was constantly trying not to offend. I am a bit surprised by this knowing that the Arab way of doing business is also very slow and careful. I mean I'd offend everyone at a business meeting here just by showing up! Dr. H is just telling me that he has released my passport and travel documents, when another Saudi doctor in full Arabic dress interrupts us. He enters the small office with his arms outstretched; a waft of some overpowering perfume assails my nostrils as he passes, ignoring me. I take my leave as they begin the prolonged kissing and hugging that forms the usual greeting before the combined fumes asphyxiate me!

Col arrives to speak with Dr. Muktar who heads our Pathology lab then we meet for lunch. We are forced to sit in the male cafeteria there being no actual restaurant in this hospital for '*married*' staff. We are a novelty and afford many interested glances. I wave my left hand around and make sure my wedding ring catches the light. We may be married but no one else knows that.

After Col leaves I rush to the admin office to collect my passport using Dr. Hammad's 'permission to release' document and exchange the gate pass for my passport and *aqama. A* telephone call comes through when I'm back in the office telling me to collect my *holiday pay*. It is in fact only my December pay paid out early but obviously makes them feel generous. An overweight Filipino official sits in the finance office behind a long narrow desk on which several piles of Saudi Riyaal's rest in towering bundles. A Saudi official sits next to the Filipino but merely watches as my salary is counted out in front of all the other Filipinos who are also waiting for their salary. I am acutely embarrassed by this (unnecessary) display of insensitivity and grab the notes trying to stuff them quickly into my pockets. My cheeks burn in indignation. They earn less than a quarter of my salary.

Delia and Lindy discuss this and other insensitivities in her apartment later. Delia hands round glasses of her best homemade coffee liqueur and we continue our intense chat until Colin comes to fetch me. Much hugs and kisses all round. I won't see them until my return in January, *the new millennium*. Delia's eyes are watering bless her.

CHAPTER ELEVEN

*"We live in a wonderful world that is full
of beauty, charm and adventure. There is
no end to the adventures we can have if
only we seek them with our eyes open."*

Jawaharial Nehru

Christmas in Sweden via Prague

We DRIVE TO Bahrain in the land cruiser, stopping
over at customs in the middle of the long bridge. We
manage to hold everyone up with all our luggage and
cameras but the process goes without a hitch, which is
great for customs in any country, never mind the Middle
East. I gaze out of the car window as we approach the
end of the causeway into Bahrain. The sea is a lovely

aquamarine colour and the air seems somehow fresher and cleaner than Saudi, a mere twenty kilometres away. Flags flutter all along the roadside on flagpoles and walls and many buildings, especially the distinctive red and white Bahraini flag. Instead of the *'royal twins'* we have the three smiling faces of the sheiks beaming down on us from lofty heights. We head along the *corniche* in Manama to check into our hotel for the night, The San Rock hotel is small, clean and not too expensive. As employees of KWMH we are entitled to a discount. We're pleased there's something to be gained from living in a Saudi compound! A laconic Filipina in a tight white shirt and short black skirt greets us unenthusiastically,

"Good *abternoohn aand welcaahm*." She intones insincerely without a smile. I get the impression she prefers wealthy businessmen to checking in families. Our room has a double bed, TV and a well stocked bar fridge and a sea view.

We freshen up and head off for *Al 'Arin*, the Bahrain wildlife reserve. It's closed till Monday. Today, of course is Friday, sod it! Al Arin Wildlife Park is the only Nature Reserve in Bahrain. We have heard that the park, the only one in Bahrain, is more than eight square kilometres. It has a few Arabian mammals and birds. We want to see the Arabian Oryx, which looks similar to our Gemsbok back home, only a lot paler. We drive on down the *corniche* and manage to find the British Businessman's club. Col shows his card and we're allowed in (after the usual search under the chassis for bombs with a mirror mounted on a pole) They are serving a buffet dinner, which looks nice as we pass the long trestle type tables laden with festive fare. We take a seat near the back of the room and place our order with a thin Indian waiter with long greasy hair.

There are many British families eating in here today judging from the thick English accents that dominate the room. Tim finds *a friend* to play with and they disappear to a nearby playground. So easy being young! Col and I don't find any playmates so we catch up on Saudi gossip instead. I can't believe we are drinking a real bottle of beer each but the Saudi presence is still strong and I find myself waiting for a tap on the shoulder. A short drive around Bahrain follows lunch and we arrive back at the hotel in the early evening and decide to go to bed early, feeling tired. We have to be up and away by 2am so I set my watch alarm. Tim isn't as tired as we are unfortunately and he wriggles around between us for nearly an hour before dozing off, pinning each of us to the bed with both arms which is doing a very good impression of a concrete slab, the bed that is. The pillows are a matching cement brick. There we lie, too tired to move and too uncomfortable to sleep. I get an attack of giggles at around 11pm. When Col asks what the awful smell is, I suggest it's the loo and he says we must be in *'Pongrain'* then. I get up for a wee but can't find the loo lights so have to feel my way around and knock over a chair in the process. We eventually give up, get up and get dressed at 1am. I defiantly order tea from room service, which costs us SR15 each! We stagger to the car with our entire luggage and a still sleeping Tim. It is very windy and quite cold at this hour. As we drive round the island towards the airport I notice everything is lit up with twinkling electric lights. It feels like being part of a giant Christmas tree.

I discover in the bright unforgiving lights of the airport toilets how horrendous I look. My jacket is *splodged* with old grease and dirt spots from our last hash camp, my white top is a crumpled mess, my boots are dusty, my jeans are tight and my hair is doing a good impression of a bottle brush. Even our grubby luggage, looks suspect. Col keeps offering me his jersey, which has little to do with concern for my warmth, and everything to do with the undignified picture I cut. Not that he looks any better mind you! We are the Swiss family *grubbins*! I buy some eye shadow and four magazines after coming through customs, which I will devour, on the plane (the magazines not the eye shadow!) Our plane is a Czech airbus and the décor is slightly tired and worn, which is not a good look for a long flight. Personally I like my planes to be perky and new—so much more reassuring! I visit the toilet at around 6am. The sign above the toilet says *flushenski,* which I do with gusto. I love watching the little dribble of bright blue water rim up and away with the flush accompanied by a sound so loud it could wake the dead. We are now apparently two hours behind so that whilst my watch assures me it is 9am I know it is really only 7am in Europe. I may get back two hours of much needed sleep.

Later Colin leaves his seat to join Henry for breakfast which is scrambled egg wrapped up in a sort of pancake. Looks weird but tastes OK which is all that matters I suppose. There is also a pale sausage of unknown origin and some chopped up pieces of fruit. Henry works in KWMH as a cardiac technologist. He is an affable man with a reddish complexion and blond hair. For me, there is the usual tea saga. Why am I doomed! I ask for tea and it comes to me black. I ask for milk and I get a lemon. So when the refill lady comes around I ask for coffee with milk. I get it black. I'm sipping the bitter stuff tentatively when the tea lady comes around again. She asks if I want more tea. I say, 'Yes please. With MILK please'. I try not to sound too edgy or put too much stress on the syllable. As she hands me the cup it is dark and milk-less. I quickly ask for orange juice and end up with two cups of black tea, one cup of black coffee and a glass of orange juice. They give me wide berth after this. Col returns to his seat.

"We'll see if the story of free accommodation in Prague is true," he says clicking his seatbelt into place.

"What's with all the fluids?" he asks peering at my assortment of beverages. "Never mind." I snap. I am so tired I could lie down in the aisle and go straight to sleep. Just before landing, the airhostess comes around handing out warm facecloths with long silver tongs. I wipe my groggy face a couple of times, removing most of my eyebrows in the process. I now look distinctly odd so when the flight attendant returns to collect the facecloth and finds me cleaning my dusty shoes with it, I am not given the usual hostess welcome smile. We meet up with Henry in the airport restaurant in Prague. He is also going to the Hotel Kladno.

Prague is the capital and largest city of the Czech Republic. Henry has been here a few times. He orders two teas and a coffee with practiced ease and I'm thinking he will be a useful chap to have around. My tea costs an arm and a leg and the milk is extra but I'm determined to get a decent cup. I notice a sinister number of witch puppets and decorations dotted around the airport Duty Free section. They must be something symbolic as it's not even Halloween.

We are indeed to be accommodated for free. Henry joins us later and the four of us take a bus, courtesy of *Czech airlines,* to Kladno where the hotel is located twenty kilometers from Prague and fifteen km from Ruzyně airport. I'm not thrilled by the name *Kludno* (sounds *cloddy*) and as we drive up to the hotel I fear I may be right. It looks small, poky and definitely *one-star* from the front. There is a dusting of light snow around the bleak countryside not unlike a mild case of dandruff and the air is distinctly chilly. We move our luggage quickly into the entrance of the lobby, which houses a long narrow counter with a glass section underneath displaying dusty wares for sale. We are given our room keys and arrange to meet Henry later. The room is small and slightly musty but adequate. It has a roof balcony sprinkled with snow. Tim wants to go outside so we quickly unpack and find our thermals, dress warmly and take a look outside on the cement balcony. I leave a few beer cans in the snow outside our window to keep cool. Dressed in every bit of warm clothing that we own, we troop down and have a look outside. We are hoping there may be a bank around but we are too far from the city for this amenity. Tim and Col have a quick snowball fight then shivering in the cold, return to the hotel to meet Henry in one of the three restaurants. The room is an awkward diamond shape with three low tables set with dry looking rye bread and empty plates. We chose a table near an open window, which is a mistake, as it sends blasts of frigid air onto my back. Our waiter is slightly overweight with dark greasy hair and a large silver earring in his left ear. He bustles up and down the small room serving watery cabbage soup. After this we are served Pork and potatoes, which is quite tasty and some hot pudding and pale custard, which is not.

We take a look around the local shops, which are a few meters down the road, accompanied by Henry, but there isn't much to see. A nearby shoe shop has some nice looking specimens in the grimy window but none of us are inspired to part with any *shekkels* so we end up taking a taxi to *Prava* town centre. The taxi deposits us outside the underground train terminus and we buy tickets to the town centre. *Avni nadrazi* is the biggest and busiest railway station in Prague. I find an irritable looking man with heavy Slavic features selling peanuts in the doorway to the station. He isn't too happy with my lack of change or that I can't speak Czech for that matter. Cold blue-knuckled fingers reluctantly pass me a wad of change. '*Děkuji moc*,' pronounced 'Dyeh-koo-yi-motzs' (thank you very much) then he turns up his collar and looks away miserably. We find a seat on the tube and rock our way into the city centre. As we step outside the train station I see it has snowed some more since we left the hotel. The air is cold and crisp and the fresh snow cracks underfoot. The city is quite pretty with twinkling lights brightening up the otherwise dull afternoon light. Prague has a busy city centre within walking distance of the main attractions. Prague Castle is on one side and Wenceslas Square on the other, with the old town across the famous Charles Bridge. There are many beautiful old buildings in Prague and I strain my neck looking up at them. Christmas decorations abound every shop window.

It is very picturesque. We find an indoor craft market and enter, our combined breaths steamy in the warmth of the building. Henry likes crystal, Prague is famous for its crystal and we have a look at their ornaments gleaming brightly in the dim light. It is readily available here and relatively cheap if you know where to go. Henry does. The stalls sell coats, hats and scarves, witches on brooms (what's with all the witches!) puppets, and an assortment of red and gold Christmas decorations. Henry takes us to a stall selling *gluhwein* and we buy a small paper cup each and wander down the street sipping the hot spicy red drink. The streets are full of people, walking, talking and drinking like us. Col buys me a long white scarf, which is very welcome and helps to keep a strong breeze from chilling my neck. Tim sees a Shetland pony and insists on having a ride. We try and dissuade him but he's insistent—that is until it's his turn to get on. Suddenly Mr. *brave heart* turns into *general Custer*. Col buys him a set of postcards and asks him to start writing a story about his holiday. That and a small packet of biscuits seem to do the trick. We walk into a warm little side shop and come out with two small pottery coffee mugs. Tim buys himself a bunny balloon, which is appropriate given his nickname. Buskers line the streets playing an instrument and singing or dancing.

The taxi driver wears a typical bushy handlebar moustache and he's listening to old Beatles music as he drives the long dark road back to the Kludno hovel, er hotel. I hum along tunelessly. Back at the hotel we leave an exhausted Tim in bed and meet downstairs for supper. This time we have potato and onion soup, steak and vegetables with another steamed pudding. Our waiter has a habit of plonking the plates down with a sibilant, "*Yesss,*" so we have, "Soup, *yesss*." followed by, "Steak *yesss*" and so on. Henry has brought a bottle of wine with him and we have a few glasses of *red* with the meal. A very pleasant end to the day, I think draining my second glass of wino. It is very warm in the room this evening. Even though the beds only have a thin cover over the sheets none of us are cold so I'm thinking they have a very effective central heating system. I get up and have a look outside. There is now a thick blanket of snow lining the verandah. The evening has that cold still air that accompanies a night of snow. I take a few deep breaths, freeze my bronchioles and have to hop into a hot shower in order to breathe again.

Tim is sitting at the table for breakfast this morning with Henry. They are chatting away twenty to the dozen. He has already eaten two rolls and drunk a cup of hot chocolate. Col and I have, "*Hum en eggsss*" courtesy of 'Gollum', which is very tasty. I dab my chin with a cloth napkin and ask the waiter for some tea. I should have known better. A tray appears with four small jugs of hot, not boiling, water and two teabags. No lids, no sugar, no milk. I call our sibilant friend over,

"Excuse me," I begin politely, "May I have some milk for my tea?" I get an answering "*Yess*" but nothing appears. Eventually I ask Henry to ask him. He appears to have what it takes as a little milk jug and some boiling water arrive soon after and the tannin depleted side of me is happy.

We chat to Henry in the small lounge until the bus arrives a little after 11am. Our luggage is taken to the hold and we board the bus for the airport. I try again to buy a cup of tea with milk but am again thwarted. I receive instead a mug of hot black coffee. I'm starting to feel a little paranoid about my tea requesting abilities. Col reassuringly puts it down to my being strange and partly British. We chat till take off then shake hands with Henry as the call for boarding is announced. He's taking another plane out to the UK to visit his wife. We board a small Czech 737. They have placed tiny Christmas decorations in all the portholes, which gives a pleasant festive air to the flight.

Arlanda airport in Sweden at around 3pm is already dark and cold and the air is crisp and fresh. *Farmor* (literally *father's mother*) and Sven-Erik meet us and we settle our things into the boot of the car and set off for Stockholm. It seems to have snowed more here than in Prague. As we drive past the typically Swedish red and white wooden houses, the traditional lights glow prettily in all the windows. I vow to buy myself a set of electric 'candle-shaped' lights for our window back home. The evening meal is typically Swedish consisting of salmon, boiled potatoes, and salad finished off with *lingonberry* cream and saffron cake. Yum! Lingonberries (*Vaccinium vitis-idaea*) are the Scandinavian equivalent of English strawberries. Found in low evergreen shrubs throughout Sweden, they are a tasty tart treat.

We have a wonderful Swedish Christmas with the family and see in the new millennium without incident or bugs of any description! All too soon it is time to say our goodbyes on 6th January and we leave Sweden for Saudi with a stop again in Prague. It is warmer than when we arrived a few weeks ago and the snow has all but melted. We have a long wait for the bus to Ludno. We stay at the same hotel, but have a different and somewhat nicer room this time. Tim, Col and I go downstairs for supper. Boiled ham and cabbage on the menu, no surprises there then! We don't sleep too well but manage to get up, dressed and be ready by 8:30am for breakfast, which comprises dark rye bread, *rohliky* (yeast rolls), salami and cheese. There is a variety of yoghurt as well.

It is a bright day with a weak sun but remains cold. We are in town and decide to walk across the famous Charles Bridge with its crumbling arches and copper statues, which line its length. There are a number of artists sitting alongside their displayed paintings. Many have painted the bridge itself and I am tempted to buy one and would if finances allowed—but alas they don't! Charles Bridge is one of the many monuments that were built during Charles' reign but it is not the first bridge that ever connected the Prague banks of the Vltava. I read something of its history written in copperplate on the side of the bridge wall. Another bridge used to stand in its place—the Judith Bridge, which later collapsed in a flood in 1342. The Charles Bridge used to be the most important connection between the Old Town, Prague Castle and adjacent areas until 1841 as it was the only means of crossing the river Vltava. This connection made Prague important as a trade route between east and west Europe. The bridge was originally called the Stone Bridge but has been the *Charles Bridge* since 1870.

We walk to the town square where the famous gold painted clocks are situated in the clock tower to one side of the square. I stand and gaze up at the beautiful work of art. Prague is a crazy quilt of architectural styles. Gothic cathedrals tower over churches. Art Nouveau are stitched alongside Cubist buildings. Clock towers abound and is partly what Prague is famous for, the oldest being on the sidewall of the Old Town Hall. This ornamental timepiece tells not only the time but symbols of the zodiac show the course of the heavens; we're informed by a small tour group leader who we've sidled up to. When the bell tolls, windows fly open and mechanical apostles, skeletons, and *sinners* begin a ritualistic dance of destiny. No-one can place this beautiful clock in time which is rather ironic. The Old Town Square is one of two main squares in the city centre (the other is Wenceslas, a five minute walk away). The Old Town Square started life as the central marketplace for Prague in the twelfth century. I didn't hear any more because at this point the tourist guide looks up and frowns at my deliberate poaching of her talk. I turn my gawping slack jawed mouth into a yawn and toddle off to find Colin and Tim.

"It's time for lunch," announces Col looking at his watch. "We don't have too much time left," he continues striding on ahead, "let's look for something close by." We walk a little further and come to a quaint little cellar type restaurant off the street. The restaurant itself is reached by walking down a winding stone staircase to the inner sanctum. We seat ourselves at a wooden table with benches on either side. A waiter appears and thrusts a huge menu into Col's hands. He misses the perplexed look on Col's face and babbles away in Czech. As my knowledge of Czech vocabulary is limited to 'thank you very much' I try a few tentative words in school—girl German instead and manage to make myself understood. I order the fresh trout for Col straight from the Vlata River (actually I just ask for fish and just HOPE its fresh from the Vlata river). Tim and I have cold meats and a cheese platter. This repast is washed down with frothy pale ale in tall glasses. We have some fun trying to work out the bill in *groats and Czech crowns.* After this pleasant meal we take a short walk up a hill overlooking the town and bridge, stopping briefly outside a beautiful building with copper turrets and railings. This building is close to the castle. There is a lot to see in a short time; swans and ducks on the river, castles, restaurants, old buildings, souvenir shops and other tourist traps, magnificent churches with steeples, and lots more.

Rushing back to the hotel via train and bus, we are just in time to see the airport bus starting up its engine outside the hotel entrance. We heave our luggage on board and settle down for the drive back to the airport. Some of the tenement buildings aren't very nice and remind me of the poorer places in London. The snow has started to melt and has turned the surrounding area to grey slush.

We meet Henry again in Dammam airport early next morning. He helps us get the Toyota battery started and we give him a lift to his compound, which is a mile out of Al Khyber. We get to KWMH at 7:15, We have left absolutely no time between returning from our holiday to starting work again so I immediately phone for a taxi, have a shower and put on my uniform. Col has already gone to work. Not feeling too great. Grant greets me at the education building and he gives me a kiss on the cheek. Besides Ding, he is the only one around. Lindy is still on her holiday somewhere with Len. Eid started yesterday which explains the general quietness in the hospital. I drag myself through the morning and am glad to get back home so I can have an early night. Tim stays up to watch cartoons and puts himself to bed. Up early again, feeling slightly better. Tim crawls into bed with us saying he's had a nightmare and doesn't want to stay home alone today.

"What was your nightmare about?" I ask stroking his hair gently.

"I don't want to talk about it now," he answers solemnly, "I'll tell you later when I'm over it." We laugh. He sounds so grown up for a six year old sometimes. However Tim's reluctance to be alone is a problem for us as well. Col has to sit around in his office waiting for the blasted prince Sultana to arrive (IF he arrives) and I have to go to work. Even if I were 'sick' I'd have to go in and be seen by Dr. *Tentacle*! I have quite a job convincing Tim it will be OK for him at home for a short while. I hate, hate, hate doing this.

Although work is quiet I don't get the chance to phone Tim before 2pm. He sounds OK and says he's had some company for an hour or so. Col wasn't able to leave his office because Prince Sultana didn't feel like seeing any Westerners today.

Chapter Twelve

"To my mind, the greatest reward and luxury of travel is to be able to experience everyday things as if for the first time, to be in a position in which almost nothing is so familiar it is taken for granted."

Bill Bryson

Saudi Exhibition

WE MEET UP with John and Nicci, Peter the Czech, Anthony and two girls all the way from Aramco and head towards Khurais and the Tuwaiq Mountain. We are going camping again for the weekend. I have to get out of the car halfway there for a wee stop, in both senses of the word! We find a good spot to camp between the amazing red sand dunes and pitch the tent as quickly as we can by the light of the moon. Anthony has a huge bonfire set up and before long we are all sitting around its glowing warmth swopping Saudi stories and sipping on home made coffee liqueur (is there any other kind here) The night is extremely cold and the ground hard and cold so I don't sleep too well. This morning we wake up stiffly and take a look at each other and burst out laughing. Cols hair is standing up in stiff sandy tufts, mine looks like a nest. We both have huge bags under our eyes. After breakfast we drive to the nearby *Musmak* fort. King Abdulaziz apparently had it built in 1930. Two guards are leaving as we arrive so we are able to have a good look around at the mud walls and huge pillars and crumbling roof without too much trouble. We circumnavigate the fort area and find an old well with herb bushes and bits of old pottery. After lunch the boys play on the dunes in their land cruisers. Tim wants to join Anthony driving down a huge dune because, "Daddy isn't brave like you"! Later Anthony takes us to a place to look for shark's teeth. I can't believe it when I find one. Col also finds a fossilized tooth, but it may well have been one of mine! We also find some more fossilized clamshells and a piece of coral. It's quite something, for a desert. We return to camp and have some tea, take down the tents and head back for the compound. We pass a huge caravan of camels and stop to take photographs. I am astonished to find out that even so far from the city, the Bedouin camel herdsmen who are dressed in *thobe* and red and white chequered *ghutra* are in fact Pakistani's. No locals are willing to herd the camels anymore now they have foreigners to do it for them.

Today we have workmen in to see about some burst water pipes in the apartment. Col has to leave Tim as he has an urgent case to see to and on his return he sees the workmen are gone, the carpet is a mess and Tim has signed the worksheet! How is it they feel it's OK for a six year old to sign a document! Tim however, is very proud to have been asked and says he drew a, "Squiggle just like daddy's!"

I have an interesting Fire prevention meeting today with June from trauma, Leanne the DON, a local fireman and a doctor form emergency room—ER. It is interesting because we're given a video on fire prevention to show at the forthcoming exhibition and asked to take a look for suitability. It is going well until an attractive woman wearing a bikini is seen drowning. This causes a minor ripple throughout the table, though probably for different reasons.

"*La, la!*" says Al-Saftie the chief fireman emphatically shaking his head.

"She must cover up!" he declares somewhat unreasonably given that it's an international film. We all look astonished.

"She should wear *abaya* and veil." continues Al-Safdie who apparently doubles up as controller of virtues. In any event he insists this one won't be tolerated in Saudi so the video is scrapped. They don't have another one. The meeting has no direction, no minutes and no sense. Everyone talks at once and the planning is non-existent. I am glad, once the meeting is adjourned, to have the silent taxi driver back home today. His bile yellow towels that drape the seats don't jar as much as the meeting did.

Col's gate pass for entry to my hospital was taken from him yesterday when he came to collect me. This morning we try and find Col's ID so I can get the gate pass renewed. The taxi driver causes a rumpus at the gate so the security guards remove *his* aqama. I shout at them all as this means I'll be late for work again. They return his *agama* but take his ID. I meet up with Dr. Al-Hammad for a quick meeting and manage to speak to him rather than his reflection for a change as he's in religious mode at the moment. He wants me to find out if I can order some medical journals online. I tell him I'll give it a try and am rewarded with a cold tissue-wrapped can of mango juice. Wish he'd get some new flavours! I take the opportunity of using the computer by drawing up birthday invitations for Tim's 7th birthday party which will be held on Pearl beach this weekend, *ins'Allah!* On the way to the printer I discover that the emergency fire exit in our department has a piece of tissue paper taped over it! No one knows why. I also hear from Victor that in the event of an actual fire we'd burn anyway because the outer door is locked and no-one knows where the key is.

I find Lindy in the corridor chatting to Leanne. She has brought 2 litres of *white paint* with her and is swinging it along as she chats to the DON. I'm horrified and worry she'll get caught. This is after all a Saudi military hospital. If caught she'd be fired on the spot! 'White or red paint' is the term expats use in place of wine. It's safer.

"Hi Janette," drawls Leanne, "How far are you with your recerts?" I draw my eyes away from the rotating plastic packet and say I'm doing fine. She's satisfied with my answer. Strange, as it's all she ever asks me but if she's happy, I'm happy. Not for long—as soon as Leanne turns away, Lindy hands me the packet and says,

"Here, brought you some wine." She may as well have handed me a live cobra. She's not very understanding when I snatch it without enthusiasm and hare off to hide it under my desk. There is a *shamaal* (warm wind) blowing when I leave work and the sky is a dusty greenish gray colour. It actually looks cold from the confines of the Toyota with the air conditioner blowing but step outside and your hair instantly lies in limp strands in the damp heat. I show Col the contents of my plastic bag and he nearly swerves off the road. He reminds me that we have four security gates to pass before reaching our local, Saudi compound.

We have another open day meeting today about the exhibition, which is to be held in a matter of weeks. There are several agendas on the go. What will be the exact day? Shall we have the entire event at the hospital or somewhere else? What will be displayed? I want to scream with frustration. In fact I want to scream period! Instead I offer to make the pamphlets once they have decided what to put in them!

A new notice pinned to the communication board asks all employees to have their blood group redone with their next *aqama* application. I'm puzzled, why do they need a new blood group? It is highly unlikely the old one will have changed I reason. Col says he had to *donate* blood before he could get *his* drivers license! He adds that the compulsory driving test he had to take was also a farce. While sitting and waiting his turn for about an hour, he noted the other (mostly Pakistani) applicants were asked to lift the bonnet of their vehicle and point out various engine parts. Col was worried. He isn't the best mechanic but after twenty minutes he had learned all the engine parts. They didn't even change the order of parts to identify. Then he was asked to complete a parallel parking. This done, he was allowed to go, clutching a Saudi drivers permit. The mind boggles.

Lindy and I have a brief meeting with Dr. H. We're back to speaking to his reflection. He likes his new tie and strokes it continuously. We tell him to look after himself and he smiles at his 'girls' concern for his health. Lindy and I take the bus into town to do some birthday shopping. Afterwards we find a quaint little coffee shop, which is accessed by climbing a set of long white painted wrought iron stairs. Our waiter courteously informs us that he doesn't have much of what is on the menu so we settle for a simple cup of tea, a cappuccino and a cheese croissant each. My tea arrives with the customary tea bag dangling over the side of the cup. Our cheese croissant has a tiny square of melted cheese on top not in the centre. They taste good though. I return to the hospital, having left Lindy behind, to ask Dr. H for Thursdays off for Lindy and myself (I had drawn the short straw). I tell him that *all* the nursing supervisors get Thursdays off. He reluctantly says we can but his left eye is twitching and he pleats his tie into a concertina of folds. His gaze is fixed firmly on his cupboard reflection or the floor and I'm not offered any juice from his little fridge. Later he pops his head around our office door and says he's not pleased that we compared our 'happy department' with the nursing department when we should know we are the 'education department (Actually *he* is the education department if you believe the sign on his door but I digress slightly). I have opened a can of worms.

"Are you not happy with me?" he asks mournfully and continues before I can answer him,

"Are *Leendeeh* and yourself not treated well?" he continues, "Do I not see to your comforts?" I am now sorely regretting I have approached the subject and try to withdraw the request but he shakes his head sorrowfully,

"No, I have given you my word that I *weel* make my staff happy and I am a man of honour." he glances momentarily into the distance considering his honour no doubt, or maybe he's remembering his last night in Holland, in any event he has agreed and I withdraw quickly in case he changes his mind. I telephone Lindy with the good news but remind her that she owes me one. Dr. Hammad, like most Saudi's, are definitely affected by the full moon. He rants and raves all morning. The classroom is untidy. I must tidy up my desk; Lindy and I need to send him reports—which we are not doing and so on. I try and avoid him for the rest of the day preferably the next week or until the moon wanes.

Thursday is Tim's birthday party at Pearl beach. We round up all his friends and drive there with three huge baskets of food. Tim runs off to play with his pals and I set up the food on the tables outside. A waiter approaches,

"Excuse me but Madam may not have a party on this private beach."

I look at him in dismay; there are twenty people to feed and huge amounts of food to be consumed. "Please!" I beg him restraining the urge to go down on my knees and grab the hem of his white trousers. Luckily this is not necessary. He steps back slightly and informs me that he will allow me to leave only the cakes on the table but I have to remove the rest of the food. I put everything back in the baskets and place them under the table and chairs. The food arrangements don't seem to affect the kids much as they eat whatever is available and happily dig around in the baskets for the *hidden* food. John and Nicci, Elke, John and Yvonne join us later and we spend a pleasant few hours talking until the dusk and tired children call the evening to an end.

Let me tell you about today—the dive money for the Jeddah trip was stolen last night, the water cylinder is leaking, I'm trying to sort out visas, leave and passport renewals, Tim's teacher wrote an email to say he isn't wearing the right jersey, Dr. Hammad is still blaming me for leaving the Education report on the bus last week, the taxi is late and I have a room full of people who are waiting to be recertified in CPR which they can't do properly in Saudi anyway. I NEED A HOLIDAY! This weekend will have to do as we all meet up in the desert again for a hash. Tim, Delia and I walk for an hour across the sand. There are many palms trees around and dead animals, dried out carcasses. One camel remains still has pieces of skin hanging from its ribcage and a dusty bell rope around what used to be his neck. We come across an old mud and wattle fort. It is a beautiful russet colour. Delia takes a few photos, which she later has framed, for me. The *down-downs* take place after everyone returns. Sue gives me a sentence for not listening to her at work! I gulp down the weak beer and join everyone on a blanket and watch the moon come up. I feel better.

We have a Education advisory meeting today with Dr. H at the helm. No one can decide whether to have a form passed that was agreed to in the previous meeting but which contains a spelling error. Delia is taking the minutes and we smile at every absurd word that passes his lips. Afterwards Dr. Al-Hammad is on a high for the way in which (he thinks) he handled the meeting. He joins Delia and I back to the department but keeps stopping and repeating how he'd shown them who's boss! We smile encouragingly but shake our heads as soon as he's out of eyesight. Lindy, Delia and I later share a taxi to visit the burns victim that Delia knows at our hospital. We are only allowed to look through a viewing room. Can't see much really. Naturally Delia is upset and she speaks with some of the burns unit staff. It appears this girl had lit some candles in her apartment and had left them burning when she went to bed. The candles caught light and started a fire from which there was no escape due to the archaic rule of having permanently closed windows for 'safety' reasons. She had tried to keep the flames at bay by sitting in her bath but had nevertheless received some bad burns. A neighbor had eventually heard her screams for help. In fact we also have locked windows in our apartment but

Colin was lucky to receive a special window opener or key when he arrived. It's worth its weight in gold in the compound and coveted by all who see it. This poor girl wasn't as lucky.

Lindy and I meet with Rydwaan outside the burns unit. He teaches Adult Cardiac Life Support (ACLS) at our compound hospital. Rydwaan is another shortish Filipino with a strange hairstyle. There are many of them dotted around the hospitals all with gelled, lifted, bouffant and downright weird hair. This one looks like a rug. Half of it is swept from the back to one side a la Donald. I stare at it rudely for some moments after we are introduced and think I need to introduce him to the laundry chap back in our hospital. We return to our apartment for some coffee. Delia helps sort out a few computer problems for Col and I before getting a taxi back to the Corniche centre. Today is another typical day at the hospital. Lindy goes into the AV room to scan some copies of her lecture notes. *Bictor* comes into the office and gives her a neck massage. Later on Dr. H comes into the office interrupting us mid sentence and says we must go and take a look at the empty room next door and design a classroom, library and language laboratory. Lindy and I steal a look at each other and she shrugs as if to say, 'yeah, why not! Lindy paces out measurements under the watchful gaze of Dr. H.

"It will cost about half a million to get the subcontractors in," he informs us gazing speculatively up at the roof, "But it costs a million Riyaals a month to run the pharmacy, this is cheaper than that".

"What!" I'm astonished. "Well, we'll just have to cut the pharmacy budget in half then!" He misses the sarcasm and strides into the hallway waving his tape measure.

"What about a comfort room for us?" asks Lindy. I suggest a powder pink *comport* room, which is instantly dismissed by Dr. Hammad. Rehaad joins us and tells me that Col has arrived to pick me up.

"Feel free to go now." says Dr. Al-Hammad magnanimously. I neglect to point out that it is time to leave anyway and hurry outside. Col drives to a huge Dunlop tyre place outside of town and we get the full 5 star treatment, a greasy plastic stool, a cardboard box for a table and a Pepsi each. You wouldn't get that kind of service anywhere else!

We leave Tim with Delia and Lindy at the Corniche centre and we head onto the BBA evening 'do' at Al-Hada compound. As we enter I feel immediately overdressed with my long black *abaya,* but conversely I will feel underdressed with only my evening dress with spaghetti straps. The lady of the house asks to take my coat but I say I am a bit cold and I see the quick look of surprise. I am irrationally irritated that she sees that I'm wearing an *abaya*, seeing as that is what it is and so wander into the kitchen to look for a drink. I find a disapproving waiter standing stiffly to one side of the drinks. Clearly I am to be waited on! I ask for a glass of red. We have diplomatic immunity so the booze is plentiful. It feels strangely different not to be drinking our *plonk* out of a plastic bottle. I chat to a teacher who has just come from Tobago and is missing her pet armadillo! The food is a delicious buffet spread of local and imported delicacies but with the general crowd permanently milling around the tables I find I can't get to it more than once and spend an uncomfortable half hour clutching an empty plate with five cocktail sticks and three olive stones. I spot Col chatting to someone against the far end of the room and move over to join him. He's talking to Peter Creighton who informs us he invented the first underwater camera using a box brownie, and a glass vase attached to a long gardening glove! We leave at 11pm and pick up a tired Tim from his adopted aunts. He has a chocolate covered nose and is clutching a drawing book and crayons.

Today is Valentines Day. My taxi driver notices my Celtic cross earrings and he brings out his rosary from a secret place under the glove compartment. He becomes quite animated as he speaks of his wife and seven children who live in Pakistan. He tells me the security guards will always stop a taxi if they see there is a single woman sitting in it. He adds that he is missing his family. I commiserate. It must be difficult having to be away from your family for such long periods. There is a notice going around the hospital saying the celebration of valentines day with anything red, flowers, cards etc. will not be tolerated! Great fun this lot! It doesn't stop the Westerners from going round surreptitiously presenting each other with cards blazoned with red roses and bunches of flowers though.

CNN reports that: Saudi Arabia has asked florists and gift shops to remove all red items until after Valentine's Day, calling the celebration of such a holiday a sin, local media reported Monday.

Sheikh Khaled Al-Dossari, a scholar in Islamic studies, informs the Saudi Gazette, an English-language newspaper that, "As Muslims we shouldn't celebrate a non-Muslim celebration, especially this one that encourages immoral relations between unmarried men and women, ". Every year, officials with the conservative Muslim kingdom's Commission for the Promotion of Virtue and Prevention of Vice clamp down on shops a few days before February 14, instructing them to remove all the usual trappings of Valentines day such as red roses, red wrapping paper, chocolates wrapped for valentines, red gift boxes and teddy bears. They raid stores and seize these symbols of commercialized love. One florist says they deliver the flowers in the middle of the night or early morning, to avoid being caught by the ministers of Vice.

We fetch Tim from school. Chat briefly to Miss Clephane who says he is coming along nicely. She shows us a story he's written:

'*We went to the besch and poot jele fish in a holl*' Ag for a seven year old it shows promise.

Back home we find Hewa inside the tiny pantry ironing. He says *'baby'* let him in. He is back from Sri Lanka where he was visiting his family. He has brought me three sets of colourful gemstones, striped bed sheets in a lurid pink and purple colour, and he's brought a lovely long green *Madiba* style shirt for Col, who wouldn't wear it if it were the last item left in his wardrobe; but I think I'll enjoy wearing it though. What a sweet man. I make up the beds in the horrid purple sheets and he is as pleased as punch. I remove them once he's gone but I'm glad he feels his gifts are appreciated.

There's an impromptu meeting with Dr. H and Jimmy Smith to discuss the design for the classroom, library and language lab in the empty room next door. The place is a total fire hazard at the moment! The Programme Director arrives, asks a few questions and next minute we have been given the entire building to design. Dr. H is over the moon and I'm left reeling and wondering if he's lost his mind. We're none of us qualified to design anything more than a dinner menu!

"We will discuss this tomorrow" beams Dr. H happily.

As I climb into the perfumed interior of the taxi I note the plastic grass across the back seat and box of tissues between the seats. Check. It must be '*Come again*' driving. I glance in the rear-view mirror and note the thin moustache. It is! This is a favourite taxi game I play because the taxi normally just arrives and waits. There is no way of telling, when hopping straight into the back without conversation, who is driving till I check the interior. *Come again,* is so called because he has to be told everything twice and is generally '*mufee englesi.*' He stops so suddenly it clears my sinuses! I grab a tissue, blow my nose and glare at him in the rear view mirror.

"Shwai, slow, slow." I admonish him sternly. He nods sideways and honks the horn.

CHAPTER THIRTEEN

*"Perhaps travel cannot prevent bigotry,
but by demonstrating that all peoples cry,
laugh, eat, worry, and die, it can introduce
the idea that if we try and understand each
other, we may even become friends."*

Maya Angelou

The Only Tree

Today is the big day! The Hospital fire exhibition
is being held at the nearby mall. Col arrives with Tim.
Everyone is bustling around happily bristling with
enthusiasm in direct proportion to my lack of interest.
Lindy and I take our positions behind our table and dish
out, according to Ding, '*pampletts and pree pens.*' I'm

given a nurse's paper cap to wear. I feel ridiculous but apparently it looks more 'authentic'. There are many people at the exhibition, milling around in groups of black and white. I show the old CPR video and answer a few questions here and there. Prince Sultan arrives wearing a long brown and gold brocade robe. "*Bictor*' strides around taking a lot of '*potograps*' and looking very important with his Nikon around his neck. He stalks around in semi hunched positions looking for the right angle: Ding is just smiling at nothing in particular and getting underfoot. The Programme Director passes our table with the prince and both Lindy and I give him a big smile and a profuse greeting and thrust a folder of colourful 'pampletts' into his hand. His greeting is not as enthusiastic and we realize somewhat belatedly that we have displayed unseemly familiarity! The Prince's entourage returns our pamphlets saying sternly that they need to be in a proper folder for the prince. Dr. H appears in the same lurid bright green shirt and tie he has worn twice this week, because I told him he looked smart. He comes over to see his girls and says everything looks great. We man the stall for six hours and I am glad to get away from it by 4pm.

I'm in the office to collect my exit/entry visa for India today. '*Jabba the Hut*' doesn't like my photographs; I'm showing too much neck or earlobe or some such thing. He says I'm too late to change them. I am annoyed with him and tell him I did everything his department has told me to do. It turns out Col has exactly the same reaction at KWMH. It is almost as though they resent your going on holiday. We both reluctantly have our photographs redone.

There's a horrid smell of incineration hanging over the office today and it gives me a headache. Victor brings me some concoction to help my headache. I pour it into the rubber plant as soon as he's left. You never know what they put into these things. It had far too many unidentifiable things floating in it. The rubber plant looks perkier at any rate.

Col and I discuss what we need to do before we go on leave: there are so many variables between us that all need to move with precision and good timing; Tim's school holiday, Col's leave, my leave, Dr. Muhkta as a temporary pathology replacement, Cape Town congresses all have to fit into place like some giant jigsaw puzzle in the land of '*ins'Allah pukran*. "Ah, *maalish,*" (never mind) I think to myself, "It will all work out, . . . *Ins'Allah*!"

DR H

Al-Hammad is in *'lunar mode'* again wandering around muttering to himself, wearing his *thobe and ghutra*. Talking to us and forgetting what he's said, rearranging his office etc. We should get paid today but rumour has it, it won't happen until after Eid, *Ins 'Allah*. Arghhh!

Lindy has had a job offer over at our compound hospital. She asks Dr. H to write her a letter of *no objection* to leaving our hospital and working at KWMH. He isn't happy and says he won't sign it, that it isn't right for 'his girls' to desert him. Hello, I'm still here! Later we have a laugh of a meeting about the extension plans. Lindy and I keep trying to suggest that we have a window in the building. They don't appear to listen.

"What about a bit of air?" I ask at last. Everyone turns to look at me for a moment as though I had broken wind then carry on discussing the library and where one would get the medical journals. My shoulders sag, defeated! I'm writing the minutes though so I quickly jot down that our suggestion for a large picture window was voted favourably. That will teach them, I think savagely. Dr. H leaves in the middle of the meeting and doesn't return. It must be Eid. Later Lindy and I leave for the bank. We have some tea at Alyssa souq near the water feature. I watch a large Saudi man chatting for ages on his cell phone and marvel again at the clash of cultures—modern and ancient literally cheek by jowl. We return to the office. Dr. H comes in and out. He's being evasive about his movements. I need to speak to him about doing his 'butt' for my holiday or I'll 'squeeze' him (to borrow his jargon) but he remains elusive.

I take Lindy with me on the KWMH hospital bus ostensibly to speak to Rydwaan regarding the ACLS course but she leaves soon after for the Corniche. I meet up with Rydwaan on her behalf. His hair has reached new heights so to speak and I find myself staring at it in fascination. I tell him I will submit his name to Dr. H for assisting with CPR at the Hospital and his hair trembles with gratitude.

"*Thahnk yew por yor assisstahnce Leendee.*" I don't bother telling him my name is Janette, it will add credence to Lindy's story should Dr. Hammad ask.

Col and I meet up for lunch in the 'married' section of the hospital restaurant.

We continue our discussion about the impending holiday and both agree it takes so much effort trying to organize and co-ordinate a vacation from Saudi as a family that you actually need to extend the leave by the time it comes around.

I have a blow out this morning. That is, my taxi does. It suddenly swerves across four lanes of traffic and comes to rest halfway up a kerb. I get out so that the driver can change the tyre, which he does with practiced ease. The second incident of this nature in a couple of weeks. I am both shaken and late for work and have to sneak in through the Admin building. Lindy later takes me to a posh restaurant near Tammimi to recover (well that's my excuse and I'm sticking to it). It is on the 9th floor by way of a small-mirrored lift. As we enter the restaurant an enthusiastic blue-eyed, pale skinned Syrian lad immediately shows us around. The restaurant is long, running the length of a series of picture windows with a great view of the town. We are probably the only people he's seen all day. He leads us to a table laden with silver crockery and starched napkins. Tall leather menus are thrust into our hands.

"We have buffet today." he beams. Buffet is pronounced *boofette.* I open the menu and do a double take,

"Hell, Lindy, take a look at these," I hiss gesturing at the right hand column where prices are neatly typed in gold ink. Both the price and the wilting fruits under a glass counter nearby put us off. It is SR 80 each for hard cheese, Laban coated vegetables congealed scrambled egg and a string of strangely shaped brown sausages. A large man in a white jacket that strains over his paunch beams over at us from behind the counter. He must be the cook and I stifle a sudden urge to giggle at the absurdity of the situation. Lindy and I sitting in our white-jacketed uniforms at a 5 star restaurant in Saudi during work time.

"We could be health inspectors." I whisper to Lindy who giggles behind her menu. That gives her an idea and she stands up and approaches the hovering waiter,

"Here are our business cards," she says enigmatically thrusting two into his hand. 'We will be back.' she promises somewhat darkly and we flee the room, press for the lift and spend the next five minutes snorting with laughter.

"Phew, got out of that one just in time." she says shoving our homemade business cards back into her jacket pocket.

"Come on then,' I suggest as the lift touches ground floor with a slight jolt, "let's go and get us some Tammimi freebies." We head towards the centre bypassing the many CD stalls that have sprung up all over town selling pirated copies of just about anything. They all appear slightly uneasy this morning.

"Microsoft have threatened to close them all down." explains Lindy nodding towards one side street where the CDs are piled high on rickety wooden tables.

Col has to see a Princess today about a strange looking mole on her neck. She is the Prince's middle daughter, I think. Everyone is nervous but especially Col. He has heard that they don't take lightly to bad news! Poor thing leaves for work with polished shoes, wearing his best shirt and tie. It turns out to be a benign cyst and everyone gives a collective sigh of relief. The hospital *top drawer* are all there to congratulate Col as though he personally saw to it the mole would be harmless. They sit in the office with the Princess sipping cardamom tea. Col says she is very pretty and he would have enjoyed the experience more if it hadn't been about a potential skin cancer. Chaz tells us later that one of the local surgeons in Jeddah stopped in the middle of his operation for prayers! The anaesthetist had to keep the patient under for half an hour longer than was necessary. Luckily the anaesthetist was Syrian as it would have been a different story if he'd popped off to pray as well. Col says one of the doctors has just had triplets (actually his wife did). He tells everyone in the tearoom that he has two children. The third child has had the *evil eye* cast over it. To mention three apparently casts aspersions on his guilt for whatever rule he has transgressed. Can't fathom this place; they are educated people but traditions run deep I suppose.

I hear another amusing story from big Sue this morning about Saudia Airlines. One of their planes took off from Dammam recently. It had some engine trouble shortly after takeoff so it returns to Dammam so they can see what the problem is. After an hour the plane tries to take off again but the officials are preventing take off as all the passengers now have *expired* exit/entry visas. They are allowed only one entry/exit per flight so the unexpected return has caused problems. The passengers have to cough up for another exit visa before being allowed to re-board the plane.

Today my Pakistani taxi driver is showing signs of inner turmoil and rage that threatens to erupt and boil over. There is much sighing and glowering at me through the rear view mirror with narrowed red-rimmed eyes. His hands clench and unclench against the wheel. I'm just wondering whether to open the door and leap out of the car when he screeches to a halt outside of gate one and virtually shoves me out of the car. One imagines if he had an ejector seat he'd have used it! I stagger in to face my room full of people awaiting recerts. One of them is an Indian doctor with a thin moustache and a shock of thick hair that rises from his forehead like a statement. He works methodically through the steps for CPR then turns to me and states seriously that he, '*vil now verk troo* the *wictums wital* signs.' I manage to hide my smile, but only just.

I arrive at work this morning to discover I had forgotten to lock the front door when leaving yesterday. The others are all huddled together asking questions. It seems four computer keyboards were taken. I find this rather strange, why only the keyboards? I try to find out what has happened but everyone just averts their eyes and say they don't know. Eventually Mohammed, the Muttawa, takes pity on me and tells me that Security took the keyboards as some kind of warped punishment for leaving the door unlocked. For nearly three hours no-one can do any work without them. I look for Dr. H but he isn't anywhere to be found. Later at home Lindy phones me and says Dr. Hammad is in a flat spin about the unlocked door. I am fed up and worried in equal measure.

This morning Dr. H tells me how disappointed he is in me. He rants on and on about the security issue in a military hospital and the unlocked door. Eventually he says I must go and apologize to security and give them a letter describing what exactly happened. Well, that is the easy part, I left for home and didn't lock the door, there's no huge secret there. I hand the letter to Colonel Al-Hadada and wait while he reads it with pursed lips and furrowed brow. I want to scream, 'Get on with it and give me my punishment'! He chastises me like a ten year old and I feel angry. I later concur it *was* irresponsible of me to leave the door unlocked in a military environment. I have a documentation workshop and rush around getting everything ready. I pass Dr. H in the corridor and he continuers with his ranting about the blasted door. He says they want to give me a warning letter. I continue with the workshop until a knock on the door announces Lindy. I am in the middle of telling her about the door incident when suddenly she pulls me into an awkward embrace and says,

"A tree has fallen onto Colin's car, I'm sorry."

"What?" my head is spinning. What is she on about?

"Jan, a tree crashed on top of the land cruiser"

My heart is in my mouth trying to take everything in.

"What tree? There aren't any trees where we live, well not many!"

"Is he alright?" She shrugs, "I don't know, I'm sorry, I just heard from Rehaad who got a phone call from someone at KWMH who was looking for you."

"Take over my class please." I ask rushing past her and nearly knocking over Dr. Al-Hammad who is coming down the corridor towards the lecture room.

"Your husband is not badly injured, *al-humdillilah.*" He tells me seriously,

"You must not think God is bad for punishing you for what you did yesterday. Please go to your husband now." he strides off and I feel weak with relief and suddenly I see the funny side—I leave a door unlocked and everyone thinks God has punished me by letting the only goddamn tree in the entire compound fall on Col's car! I find myself laughing. Wiping the tears from my eyes I inform a startled Lindy, who has found me laughing like a drain in the corridor, that Col is OK but I'm off home to see what the damage is. When I get there, it looks quite bad from the front; the entire roof and windscreen has collapsed and needs replacing. Luckily we are insured. Col says he'd just left the car five minutes earlier. I tell him it happened because I'd forgotten to lock the door at the hospital and he shakes his head in dismay. What a place.

"Never mind", he says comfortingly, "Tomorrow we'll be on a plane heading for India".

CHAPTER FOURTEEN

"What you've done becomes the judge of what you're going to do—especially in other people's minds. When you're traveling, you are what you are right there and then. People don't have your past to hold against you. No yesterdays on the road."

William Least heat

Whiplash

WE RETURN A few weeks later from a very interesting holiday in India. We experienced tigers and curry, crowds and several *Delhi Belly incidents* but it was all worth it. Tim's tum is a little better but the poor lamb has lost a lot of weight when he got a mild dose of Typhoid. I coax some supper into him and make sure he has an early night.

I am thrown back into things at work and by the end of today feel as though I never had leave. One of the English chaps we met last month at the exhibition, Tony Hall calls us at work. He invites Lindy and I for lunch tomorrow. He's a lecturer at the nearby university and says he wants to chat to us about a work proposition. Lindy and I are quite intrigued but we have to wait for tomorrow lunchtime. Tony arrives on time. He phones our office number and we sneak outside to meet him. He is waiting around the corner from the office. Lindy hops in the front with him and I climb into the back of his car. He is a small man of around forty-two or three years of age, conservatively dressed in beige trousers and short-sleeved shirt and tie. He wears spectacles and a slightly ruddy complexion and has short brown hair. The car is hot and stuffy and the back is strewn with books and papers. I remove a diary from under my bottom and ask where he's taking us.

"You'll see," he says weaving in and out of the afternoon traffic,

"How did you manage to get through the gates?" I want to know. Even visitors have to have evidence of an invitation to get through our gates. Tony turns around to answer me, and nearly swerves into a truck,

"Oh that's no problem," he says airily. "I have a gate pass as a member of the education faculty." Lindy glances at me. We're impressed. Tony drives to a tall ten-storey building. I squint up at the sign in front, 'The Al-Quarani Hotel,' I murmur raising an eyebrow,

'Hmmm not bad.' The large entrance is marble floored and the décor full of brass and copper ornaments. Huge hanging pot plants adorn the walls. A centre table has a buffet spread out sumptuously and we waste no time piling our plates. I feel a little conspicuous in my uniform but no one else seems to notice. There are only a few other diners and I wonder what will happen to all the leftover food. The conversation is a little stilted at first as Tony asks us questions about our role in the hospital. We tell him about working in the education building and how difficult we find it to work there as no-one seems to want to be taught anything. He nods thoughtfully then the conversation takes an interesting turn.

"Do you girls want to make extra money?" Lindy's eyes light up, "Yes, of course we do. We're only here to make money." she continues forking up a large shrimp from her plate. Tony dabs at his mouth with a serviette,

"Well, I'm looking for a mistress." he says matter-of-factly and I nearly choke on my crème brûlée. At a loss for words we pretend we heard wrong and Lindy asks me to pass the salt. But Tony is determined.

"I earn a good salary," he says looking from Lindy to me to see how we react to this snippet. 'Go on.' says Lindy leaning back in her chair and giving him her full attention.

"I just need a mistress to give me a hard time." he continues taking a sip of his apple juice. I take a gulp of mine and wish it were something stronger.

"Didn't you just say your wife is living here with you?" I ask. He smiles,

"Joyce and I understand each other." Lindy and I exchange glances. Tony continues, knowing her interest is piqued.

"I have SR5000 already outlaid to pay whoever becomes my mistress." Lindy's eyes have widened and I can see she's doing a quick calculation. I clear my throat,

"By mistress, what exactly are you referring to?" Tony says quite seriously that his intention is to have a mistress who will be dominant.

"She will need to be very severe with me." He continues, "and perhaps even beat me." His eyes gleam in anticipation and Lindy and I are silent gallantly munching on our food for a few minutes, chewing over his rather outrageous offer before Lindy asks,

"How often do you need to be beaten?"

"How often would you be prepared to do it?" counters Tony.

She is saved from responding by the timely arrival of the Maître D who by all accounts knows Tony well.

"So how are you and your charming guests enjoying the meal Tony?" he enquires rubbing his hands together and winking at Tony. Lindy takes this opportunity to jump up,

"It was delicious!" she exclaims enthusiastically, "I have to powder my nose and then we have to leave." Tony nods and takes out his wallet and I stand around nervously while he pays and Lindy 'powders' her nose. Mercifully Tony says nothing more during the drive back and we chatter away nervously about working in Saudi until we arrive back at the department. Hopping out quickly I stammer a thanks and rush away before he says any more about the offer. Too late,

"Remember to think about what I said." he shouts after us before driving off. We enter the office, close the door and start laughing,

"What on earth was that!" I splutter, "Was he just asking us to become a dominatrix?" Lindy laughs, "Yes he is. And he's willing to pay quite handsomely for it". We collapse laughing at the absurdity of it all. I think of his wife either knowing or unknowingly unaware of these deviant fantasies of his. We joke about how we could go along and lash him for five minutes and run away with the money.

"SR5000 is a lot of money." repeats Lindy speculatively. I look up startled, "You're not really considering it are you?" She smiles, "I might be!" Lindy looks at her emails and sees an invitation from Ruth.

"What does it say." I ask shuffling some papers around my desk in an attempt to tidy it. "She says," and here Lindy breaks off with a giggle, "that I am invited to a lovely buffet meal at The Al-Quarani Hotel tonight!" I stare at her in disbelief,

"Are you going to go?" She nods. "Where on earth are you going to put it all!" She shrugs, "I'll do take away!"

Today is my birthday and I get a combined birthday cuddle from Col and Tim and some nice perfume. Lindy gives me some bath oils, a wooden loofah and a wallet from Len. I give the AV guys, Grant, snake and pocket billiards (Rehaad and Aziz respectively) some cake courtesy of Tammimi. Aster presents me with a computerized birthday message that he'd drawn up. Quite sweet. Lindy and I disappear to the Al-Naseem hotel and have a lovely breakfast of fruit, cheese and coffee. We sit and chat about things at the hospital then Lindy asks me what I think about Tony's offer,

"Are you serious about this?" She looks thoughtful, "well I'm only here to make money. The quicker I do, the quicker I can go home to be with my family."

She tells me that Tony has already sent her a CD giving information on what is expected of a dominatrix. It sounds too weird for me. The idea that someone would actually pay for pain seems unthinkable.

"But Linds, you are far too soft to be a dominatrix!"

"Like I said, I can do anything if it will help to get me out of here quicker."

I don't need the money thankfully but Lindy has left her family to contribute to the income as times are hard. I caution her about getting into something that she may regret.

"Why don't you join me!" she exclaims suddenly. I stare at her as if she's gone barking,

"Me? I would be hopeless. I'm a nurse remember . . . do no harm and all that."

"Well IF I do decide to go along with it, I would be happy to know you're around in case he gets violent or something."

I laugh, "Lindy, he's at least three inches shorter than either of us!" We both giggle. "We need to think of a good name for Tony so that we can talk in code at work if need be."

We come up with, *'Whiplash'* and snigger at the appropriateness of it. I leave the matter with a firm promise to be on the end of a phone if she ever needs me.

We run into Fiona at the hospital entrance. She'd seen us on the bus going to town and here I am still clutching the same envelope three hours later. I don't care—it's my birthday. I meet Delia later at the Gulf and we walk to the Olivetto hotel for supper. It seems to take ages to get there and we both have blisters by the time we get to the front steps of the restaurant. On the way we stop off at a *souq* and I buy some hipsters. It is too hot to walk and the temperature must be in the upper forties. We find a small table and order some crispy salad and a pasta dish. I go to the toilet to try on my new jeans. They won't even go over my calves. Bugger! I wish the shops would allow trying on before buying. I am disappointed but my blood supply is completely cut off at the calf so I have to change back into my old jeans. The meal is very nice and Delia and I spend a good hour chatting. We order tiramisu for pudding. Our waiter and two others bring it out. As they approach they start singing, "Happy birthday to you!" while, much to my embarrassment, a tape croons the same message nauseatingly in the background. The tiramisu bears the legend, 'Happy Birthday *Gan'* in chocolate icing. Delia laughs,

"I shoulda said your name was Janette." I shrug and smile, "Nah, then they'd just have used up more icing with the name *Ganette".* We tuck in. No wonder my jeans don't fit! I find I am on first name terms with the waiters by the end of the evening who ask me to call them variously, Mario, Ricardo, Victorio and other similar Italian sounding names. As they are all Filipino and Indian, I'm guessing they aren't their real names.

On the way home I exchange my *tourniquet* jeans for an odd knitted jersey that is both sleeved and sleeveless, collared and collarless depending on which part is attached or detached. I amuse my self with one full sleeve and a collar but it is too hot to keep the jersey on for more than five minutes no matter how many parts I remove.

I give Delia a card and some carved napkin rings as a goodbye *pressie*. Col collects me with a sleepy Tim in the back of the car. Delia and I bid our fond and tearful farewells. She and Paul are leaving Saudi Arabia for Spain in the coming week. Delia is laden down with bags and parcels from the last hour's shopping. She emails me later and says she's sure Tim's last impressions of her are of a weeping *bag lady*.

This evening I am hurriedly making supper for Doctor Ismail and his wife. They are South African Moslem and will be taking some things for us next week on their trip home. We have invited them to watch our recent video on India. They are due at 6pm so I clean and polish and cook some chicken Korma. I kick the prayer mats into a corner in case it is seen as inappropriate to use them as actual carpets. 6:30 comes and goes and no sign of them. I stir the fast congealing curry and fling some plates into the oven to warm up. At 7pm Col and I are so hungry we are ready to gnaw on our own knuckles.

"Wait just a bit longer." pleads Col. At 7pm Ismail phones us and says he's stuck at prayers but will be there shortly. I am fuming and don't even feel like opening the door to him. Col is still on the computer when they eventually arrive at ten to eight. I open the door and his wife marches in and thrusts a small bowl of soup into my hands saying she hopes it will go with the supper. I give a tight smile, invite them into the lounge and rush into Col hissing that he'd better take over as I'm going to try and chisel dried curry out of the pot for supper! In the kitchen I remove the cling wrap from the bowl of soup and peer at it. Only enough for two people so I microwave it on high for a minute or two and dish it up saying we won't have any. They sit slurping their own soup while Col and I look on awkwardly trying to hide the sounds of our own gurgling stomachs with a cough or two. His wife Soraya says she's interested in starting up some art classes so I show her some of my watercolours in miniature. We get to the third one and she stares at it for a moment before asking how long we intend staying in Saudi. Her tone alerts me that something is amiss. I glance down at the small painting in her hand. It is my cartoon caricature of some covered ladies being removed with the trash van. I gently remove the painting from her hand and mutter about supper and bring out the main dish, now thoroughly dried out clumps of chicken astride a mound of congealed rice. I place Tim's plate next to Col and we start to eat. I glance over at Tim and notice with horror that he's eating pork (courtesy of Delia's last trip to Bahrain), I get up and hastily remove the plate before they notice, leaving Tim squawking in protest,

"Sorry darling," I beam at him, "Mummy gave you the wrong meal." Tim's mouth trembles,

"But I like *pork* chops mommy." he says tears sprouting at the corner of his eyes. I set the plate down again.

"Ok, pet, you can finish off the *turkey* and rice. I'll keep your spaghetti for tomorrow." No one has bought this ludicrous attempt to disguise the forbidden meat and the rest of the meal is consumed in silence. They leave soon after that.

"Funny, they didn't even want to watch the India video." says Col who missed the whole pork episode. I retort that it must be a cultural thing and go to the kitchen in search of a little liquid refreshment. I find nothing stronger than vinegar so we take ourselves off to bed muttering about strange Moslem visiting customs. Secretly I'm thinking they must find us equally bewildering.

Tony alias '*whiplash*' phones Lindy and asks if we'd like to go for lunch. Lindy asks where he'll take us. It is Al-Nimran, our favourite café. He picks us up and takes us through the traffic in the hot car chatting about work. Lindy and I are ready to giggle like a couple of school kids, as the situation is so strange and unreal. We order lunch and chat about safe general matters. The subject of pain infliction does not come up and we are relieved if a little surprised. However the meal is good and *Whiplash* drops us off in the hot dusty street a little way from the Corniche centre where we will change out of our uniforms. We set off for the Woman's Centre. Before leaving, Tony invites us for dinner tonight at around 7pm. We accept and start walking up the street looking for the club. We can't find it at first and tempers fray in the heat. I suggest we try a little further up a side street and suddenly, there it is. We enter the doorway via a huge wooden screen into the delightful cool interior. Nadeerah meets us at the door, an attractive Turkish woman with flowing dark hair only partially hidden under a long silk scarf. She shows us her beautiful jewelry designs. I buy a silver bangle for my sister Jos who likes silver. Nadeerah also has some beautiful dresses. She invites us to a belly dancing evening tonight starting at 9pm till 2am. We take a '*rain check*' as the Americans would say.

At around 6:30 Nicci joins us near the Corniche Centre. We tell her that *whiplash* has invited us for supper (actually we call him Tony) and ask her to join us. We figure he will be delighted to be joined by three women. I am a little anxious that he may bring up the dominatrix thing with Nicci present but decide, based on lunch that he won't bring it up again. We meet him at the appointed hour, introduce him to Nicci as a fellow lecturer from the university and he drives us to the Al-Quarani. There is the usual buffet spread and Nicci's eyes light up,

"Oh wonderful, I love seafood." she says happily. There is a seafood theme this evening and soon we are all tucking into lobster, crab and shrimp with abandon. Conversation starts in a relaxed vein and we are soon laughing about funny happenings in Saudi. Then suddenly Tony says,

"So, Nicci are you also into pain?" she looks puzzled and I give a little hysterical laugh,

"Oh *Toneeeh* you joker, we're nurses! We don't like to inflict pain, we make people feel *better.*" I pat Tony's hand as though to humour his strange ways. Inwardly I imagine battering his hand to a pulp. He had better not say anything more on the subject. Nicci starts to talk about her work and Lindy and I glance quickly at each other. *Whiplash* listens politely for a few minutes then says,

"I have you as the strong dominant type." Lindy and I splutter, "Oh no silly, Nicci is as sweet as pie, a real softy nurse, aren't you Niccs, a typical loving *caring* nurse." Nicci looks in puzzlement from Tony to Lindy, then her gaze settles on my rictus-like smile. Lindy stands up and says somewhat wildly,

"Come Nicci, let's get some more of this delicious food." I lean over the table as they leave and hiss at Tony to behave or else we leave. He looks the picture of studied innocence,

"Well I thought she was game seeing as you brought her along. What else was I to think?" I am in the middle of telling him that she knows nothing of this peculiarity of his when they return to the table. Nicci chatters on oblivious to the air of tension. We have coffee and steer the conversation away from anything that involves the subject of pain—in any form! I stifle the urge to giggle thinking how ridiculous the situation is. Three nurses having supper in Saudi with a short English man who wants to pay one of us to clobber him. *Whiplash* calls a taxi for Nicci and I to take us back to KWMH I leave Lindy with him and raise an eyebrow questioningly. She shakes her head imperceptibly; "Tony is going to give me a lift back to the Corniche." We say our goodbyes and leave for the KWMH compound.

"Well that was a pleasant evening." says Nicci taking out a cigarette and lighting it. "What a funny man though. He kept on saying strange things and winking a lot to you and Lindy. Am I missing something?" I laugh wildly,

"No, ha ha no, no no, NO! Haha" I have overdone the laughter; Nicci is staring at me as though I've gone mad.

"He *is* a bit strange." I say more quietly and leave it at that. We are five minutes away from KWMH when I give a sudden start.

"Oh no!" I groan. I have just remembered that I have left my bag with my clothes, shoes, ID, gate pass and diary in the back of *Whiplash*'s car. Nicci asks the driver to turn back and chase after the others but we are too late, Tony and Lindy have long gone. Nicci tells me not to worry; I can just wear another uniform and shoes for tomorrow. I nod but she doesn't know that the real reason I'm panicking is because I'm thinking of Tony's wife and what she'll do if she discovers a nurse's uniform and shoes in the back of his car. My gate pass and ID will be all she needs to have me deported or worse. I don't buy the 'Joyce knows all about my interest' lark. I start to sweat. The taxi drops us off; I bid a hasty goodbye and leave Nicci staring after me speculatively. I dash up to our apartment; rush past Col and try to phone Lindy. No answer. I hang up the phone and contemplate my fate. The only thing I can do now is to email her and ask her to contact Tony on some pretext. She has his number, she can ask him to hide my things until tomorrow and to bring them to work. Col is perplexed when I take myself off to bed but lie tossing and turning all night. Next morning I am up and ready by 7am. I take the bus to the hospital and cross my fingers in the hope that security doesn't ask for my gate pass. We stop at Gate One and the security man hops on board and walks down the aisle. My heart is beating wildly. I hope and pray he doesn't notice anything amiss. Luckily I am in uniform. He returns to the front of the bus, hops off and waves the driver on. I exhale slowly.

Lindy has my bag of crumpled things waiting for me in the office.

"What did you guys do after we left you?" I ask pinning my ID carefully onto the front of my uniform. It seems she went shopping with him and he bought her a long tube dress in a slinky black material and some very high stilettos. She says he also bought a whip. Very scary stuff but she insists that she's just using him, will just string him along and doesn't intend to take matters any further. I'm not convinced but figure that she knows what she's doing.

CHAPTER FIFTEEN

"Wandering re-establishes the original harmony which once existed between man and the universe"

Anatole France

Gulf Sea

COLIN, TIM AND I are going to Henry's place tonight for Paul's farewell. Paul is a young English recruit that worked in the IT department of our hospital for a year. As we arrive I note the typical compound type buildings—tall, square and uninteresting. As we enter the room I can see Henry has worked very hard to make the interior as homely as possible. The walls are covered in masks, decorative silver daggers, gilt framed paintings, photos from all over the world and against one wall in the small dining room was an enormous framed jigsaw puzzle painting. There are some interesting ornaments as well, such as a comical baboon carved out of a coconut shell, a red wine bottle form Sri Lanka and different coloured glass bottles. Henry greets us warmly and offers us a *frothie* from a large plastic 'water' container on the kitchen table. Glass in hand we wander back into the living room, which is living up to its name! Music plays loudly in the background and people sit drinking and chatting animatedly in small groups in every available space. We have a lovely meal and Tim goes to sleep on Henry's bed. There are, surprisingly enough, a few locals here as well sitting incongruously in their *thobes* and *ghutras*, drink in hand. Later on a few of them get up and shuffle around the dance floor in time to the Bee Gees. Much later one of the be-thobed gents takes my hand and drags me onto the dance floor and we bop around to the music.

Today I accompany Col into town to fetch his *histamara,* a legal travel license that is required for anyone wanting to travel outside of the province. The office block where we are to meet the lawyer is the usual white brick building in a state of disrepair. A rather effeminate man wearing high waisted trousers and shiny patent leather shoes greets us at the door. He has the telltale dramatic use of hand gesture that advertises his sexual leanings. He asks us to sit and minces off to find Mohammad. His (male) secretary comes out, also in high-waisted trousers and offers us some tea. When it arrives he pours it out with his little finger raised and lips pursed. Col asks to have his *histamara* and car papers translated from Arabic to English. This takes about twenty minutes. When the document arrives back in our hands it states that '*Olle Patrick van*' wants to transport his '*Toyota golden jeepbox*' to South Africa. We thank him but Col scratches his head,

"How in hell am I going to explain this to a South African customs official!" I shrug helplessly and suggest, "Just tell them we are coming from Saudi. I'm sure this will explain everything and it shouldn't be a problem." I pause a few beats and add impishly, "*Ins 'Allah*". Colin whacks me about the bottom with his *histamara*.

"No problem, I give you free lift." says the taxi driver we've just flagged down to get to Al Rashid mall. Lindy and I spend a good hour going from shop to shop trying on makeup. We try out some samples and come out with as many *freebies* as possible for '*buffy*' eyes and wrinkles. We enter a little shop selling an assortment of items. I point out a few 'flaws' in a teapot and cup combo and get it for SR60 down from SR95. It is customary to bargain for virtually everything in Saudi. The art of gentle persuasion and negotiation is key to an enjoyable transaction for both parties. A win-win situation if you will.

We nip into a department store just before prayers. A couple of Syrian males are behind the counter. They don't seem to care that it is prayer time and Lindy and I receive the undivided attention of a salesman each. My attendant peers at my face and provides me with some free samples of an expensive skin product. Not to be outdone, Lindy's assistant brings out some freebies and hands them to her. I receive another cream for the eyes, so does Lindy. I ask for one of hers. We stagger out half an hour later with a pile of samples, a liberal spray of Chanel and a string bag each. We lean against the wall and laugh in delight. 'Let's try the internet café.' suggests Lindy as we trundle up yet another side street. We find another Syrian-run café and chat to the owner, a swarthy man in tight blue jeans and expensive silver watch. He has a long fringe over one eye, which he flicks back every five minutes. We order cardamom coffee each which is delicious, even if the temperature *is* over 45°C! We are chatting to the owner of the shop next door, a jeweler cum accessory shop, when his cousin enters the room. He sees we are in uniform and asks Lindy for advice about his acid reflux problem. As a reward she is invited to go over to his shop across the way and choose herself a gift. I then find myself diagnosing irritable bowel syndrome and the owner of the jewelry shop gives me 50% off my temporary belly button ring. I suggest a good diet and am asked to select as many stick-on tattoos as I want. I quickly select four (not wanting to appear greedy) and a small ring. I bound out with fond farewells, to meet Lindy, who hasn't done too badly either judging from the number of packets she is clutching with a huge grin, 'Look' she says opening her packet. She has acquired a cell phone cover, hands free extension and a special light switch, all for a few minutes advice! Buoyed by our success, we nip into our favourite sweet store and come out with a caraway and mint toffee, a coconut ball and a soggy honey-covered semolina ball. Flagging down a taxi, we head back to the hospital. Another day in the life!

Col and I have our passport photos taken in 'photograph' street so called as it has at least five photography shops right next to each other. A rotund

Indian leads us into a dark room in the back with his camera slung around his neck. He positions me on a high stool and makes me laugh with his,

"*Cloze yor lips, one, two tree,*" whilst flinging himself into ridiculous poses to get the 'right' picture. When it's Col's turn, he makes him wait too long—smile frozen on his face while he fiddles with his camera. Col eventually stops smiling and scowls just at the moment the photo is taken. This makes him so cross that he stomps out of the cubicle in a huff.

Back at work I nip into the dentist for my crown fitting. Only it doesn't—fit that is. The whole rigmarole of being flung upside down in the dental chair while a kilo of putty is shoved into my mouth is repeated. This after several 5-inch needles are shoved straight into my palette. He misses, and my tongue takes the bulk of the anaesthetic. He asks if my palette is numb and I reply,

"*Noh wheely, oo goh ih ih eye ungh insteh,*" while dribbling all over his wrist. Serve the bugger right, I think as he compresses a thick wad of warm wax painfully against my 'un-numbed' palette. My mouth is filling up with spit and the *eedjits* fingers are pressing against my nostrils so I am now two senses down, my arms flail wildly as I fight for breath. He tells me to breathe through my nose and seconds before passing out he releases his grip and I inhale deeply while spittle dribbles down the side of my mouth.

"This *toot* is *tempohrerreeh*," he informs me before striding out of the room to presumably duck his head under the tap. He doesn't say just how temporary, for the filling comes out, on my way back to the office. A small piece of chewing gum holds it in place for the remainder of the day. Dr. Al-Hammad is in his Western phase again and comes in wearing tight blue jeans and a pink shirt and sunglasses. Admiring his blue and red spotted tie, I try and compress my lips together to form the words,

"Ooh ook 'erry 'ice." But my thickened tongue gets in the way of every syllable. He preens into the nearest available reflective surface which happens to be my framed qualification on the wall behind my desk. Then stops and peers at me,

"What is wrong with your voice?" I open my mouth to reveal the affected tooth covered in pink gum and he quickly backs away and asks how many people I have booked for CPR before leaving. I sigh heavily, releasing another unseemly dribble onto my collar, my tongue is throbbing as the anaesthetic effect wears off. Shifting another small wad of gum under the new filling I continue writing up my nursing report for the DON.

I have just landed in Bahrain airport after a couple of weeks leave in South Africa with Tim, and I'm suffering from a mild dose of flu. This results in my becoming completely deaf from the air pressure. I spend the entire flight lip-reading the airhostesses every speech and therefore got chicken instead of beef for my lunch. Colin is still on a diving holiday in Bhutan so Len is at the airport to meet us. I am pleased to see him, as he will help smooth the way back into Saudi. Lindy has given him a long list of things to buy so we head off to a grocery store and buy about three kilogram's of bacon. The veiled Filipina woman at the till looks up and asks me if I'm travelling to Saudi, 'yes I am.' I'm not sure where this is heading but she just nods and repacks the bacon thickly in white paper before attaching a sticker that reads *turkey ham*. I smile at her gratefully. The fewer problems we have in Saudi customs the better. In any event there are no *mushkilas* and we drive through customs in the middle of the long King Fahd Causeway bridge to Dammam then on to Al-Khyber. Len drops Tim and I off at the apartment. The air smells stale and I switch on the air conditioner. As mentioned earlier, we are not allowed to open any windows in the apartment and have only the one precious *window key*.

I visit Dr. Faziem this morning as my sore throat and sniffles have worsened in the night. I present my flu-like symptoms to him and he quickly returns the verdict,

"You have the flu-like symptoms." I nod in agreement. He writes out a script, signing off with a flourish. He remembers just in time that he hasn't listened to my chest and gets his stethoscope pressed against my skin before I have time to comment.

"Ah let him have his two seconds of fun," I think charitably. It is indicated in this case. Doctor Hammad and Dr. *Who* agree I must take off tomorrow as well. Good of them I think somewhat grimly as I telephone for the taxi. I spend the rest of the day in bed and the next day we prepare for a boat trip to Jubail. Col returned from Bhutan yesterday. My cold is still giving me a thick head but I'm hoping the sea trip will clear it a little. The boat is a small 'live aboard' and the sea is rough. I pop an anti nausea pill quickly down my throat with a glug of bottled water and watch the gray, white foamed waves break against the deck. I meet a portly gray haired man in blue overalls on deck.

"Bill's, the name." He pumps my hand a few times and tells me in a strong English accent that he is an ex ship engineer from Exeter.

"I've been sailing for many years, this is rough but won't last long." He informs me confidently. He shows Tim some magic tricks. He must double as a children's clown I think watching Tim gazes in awe as yet another coin is extracted from behind his ear. Bill becomes very sea sick after half an hour's sailing and he disappears below deck to lie down. So much for the idea that captains don't suffer from seasickness. Col, Tim and I lean out over the bough getting sprayed with cold salty water. The choppy sea turns a dark gray by nightfall. I bring up a thin mattress from below deck and lie it crossways on the top deck. There are about fifteen people on board and space is at a premium. We descend to eat bacon rolls then Tim and I walk unsteadily up the rope ladder to the top deck to sleep. The position of our mattress means my head is either up or down which doesn't help my cold-thickened head at all. Col joins about eight others for a couple of night dives while I doze on and off throughout the night. I glance groggily at my watch, it's just after dawn. The light is grey and misty but it is still warm. The green baize deck covering that I slept on looks like mown grass and was just as prickly. My bladder is full so I get up unsteadily against the rocking of the boat and head for the one and only toilet. Sitting on the loo in rough weather makes for some interesting gymnastics but I manage somehow. As daylight spreads a streak of pink and lilac through the gray skies, the sea changes to a beautiful turquoise colour as we head for Jenna Island. Tim and I are paddled over to the small finger shaped island on a small rowing boat and left for an hour and a half. There is not a tree or a bush in sight just a kilometre of white sand and some rocky protrusions grouped unevenly here and there. Tim swims while I investigate the area. It is very hot and without shade becomes rather uncomfortable. I gaze anxiously over at Tim; his fair skin is already turning red despite a layer of sun cream. After an hour of walking around, picking up bits and pieces of driftwood and shells I feel the need to return to the boat and begin walking back to the drop off point to wait for it. En route I come across a beautiful yellowy—green snake with thin black rings lying motionless in the wet sand. I bend down to pick it up and add it to my collection of interesting items. My fingers curl around the tail and I realize it isn't dead! The minute my hand has returned, like a snap of elastic, to its rightful place somewhere above my head, it wriggles quickly back into the surf. Col tells me later that, from my description, it was probably a Yellow Sea snake (*Hydrophis spiralis*), and as for all sea snakes, rather poisonous!

A small boat is approaching and I call Tim over to wait with me. It turns around forty metres away and sails past. I wave my arms in a panic but it continues to sail past the small island. The tide has gone down to such an extent that the coral is exposed like the bleached bones of a grave. They glisten wetly in the strong light.

I gingerly tiptoe over a few but it is painful. Hands on hips, I gaze over at Tim and back to where I see the boat. I realize then why he hasn't come for us. The tide is so low that the boat is unable to approach closer than it has and he is trying to find a gully of water to sail along to reach us. I feel more and more anxious as I see the boat turning this way and that. I can't swim and there is no way Tim or I can get closer to the boat. I watch anxiously, the hot sun beating down on my back. I bring Tim closer to the edge, looking out for more sea snakes. Looking up, thankful to see that the boat is slowly approaching us now. The Indian moves his way slowly and carefully over the shallow water towards us, feeling the way with his oars mainly by keeping to the watery areas that are trapped between coral depressions. When he is as close as he can be without getting stuck, he shouts out for us to come. Holding tightly onto Tim's hand, we pick our way gingerly over the exposed coral to the where the small boat is gently bobbing. We step in and I flail around while the boat settles our weight.

"Thank you!" I gasp gratefully, "I know it is difficult getting the boat to us." The Indian nods sideways,

"No problem Madame." He navigates the little boat expertly back to the dive boat. Colin has been watching our progress from the bridge and hands us a towel. We sit below deck sipping tea while the boat turns back towards Jubail. An old 'Mr. Bean' movie is put on and we watch it for a while on the small screen set up for this purpose. I notice the sea is becoming quite rough again. Waves smash against the window and portholes and we bounce up and down in our chairs. The boson's chair falls over with a crash. I'm quite pleased when the harbour approaches. We unload our gear under the watchful eye of the coast guards and the occasional local who is out for the entertainment value that observing salty crumpled Westerners bring.

As we drive home Col and I chat about the causeway restaurant that we went to yesterday for an early supper. Both of us had felt vaguely depressed afterwards. The room was bare save a few strands of Xmas decorations; some paper flowers and an over decorated Christmas tree. We find it strange that they don't have any qualms about putting up a Christmas tree in a Moslem country in the middle of a causeway. They call it a, *holiday decoration.* As we ate I looked down at the dark figures of women sitting in small groups on the lawn with their children while their white robed menfolk sat apart, drinking cardamom coffee and smoking a hubbly bubbly. It appears to be an odd relationship veiled and an unenviable to the westerner. A large tinted 4X4 land cruiser drives by. As it passes under a brightly lit street lamp, the vague outline of three veiled women is revealed and I wonder what it is they think they are hiding behind their darkened windows.

Lindy and I are in town. We ask the waiter of the Al-Zair restaurant for a cheese sandwich and wait with bated breath to see what he will bring. Yesterday this request produced Arabic bread rolled around cream cheese and honey. Last week the same request brought a plate with three slices of toasted bread topped with chicken and a lettuce leaf. I open my sandwich cautiously and see some grated cheese nestling among the chicken bits. Lindy asks for a little sweet homemade toffee and fruit.

The waiter is quite taken with her charms and he thrusts a box of sweets in her hands as we leave even though I had paid the bill, which annoys me. He asks us to return anytime and bids a fond farewell. We highjack a bus and get dropped outside the hospital back entrance by 3:30. We are just in time for our weekly meeting with Dr. H. He has just returned from six weeks in Europe and is back in his *thobe, ghutra and iqal,* atoning for his sins methinks. He greets us warmly, offers us the now familiar tissue enveloped can of juice which we sip whilst he extols our virtues. I have the grace to feel embarrassed but Lindy has no such qualms and tells him how busy we've been. Ding pops his head round the door and says I have a phone call. I excuse myself and answer the phone to Len who reminds me that he's here to pick me up as planned. I return to Dr. H and Lindy. I tell him I urgently need to see a nurse in casualty (ER). He nods understandingly and I rush off to the car park to find Len waiting for me in his car, which bears the legend *Bin Laden* down one side. He takes me home and picks up the stuff he and Lindy left behind from their recent shopping expedition to Bahrain. He is meeting Lindy later on to play darts at Brian's place.

It's Thursday morning and Lindy has left early for the beach with Len. I am annoyed as *Bictor* brings a slice of cake for Lindy and a toasted sandwich from *Snake*. What am I then, chopped liver! It's seriously disgusting the way they all fawn all over you here if you are *pigmentally challenged* in the hair department. I mean they're worse here than the rest of the world. As a red head, I'm just considered a witch. Ibrahim Al-Saftie, coincidently the *safety* officer asks me to attend another exhibition. A thin man with a pencil moustache, he wears his blue overalls proudly and fiddles with his collar as he speaks. We are discussing the next fire and safety exhibition. There is no plan, objective, or any particular order but I am expecting as much and am not disappointed. The room is thick with *Ins 'Allah's* and hot air. They want everything set up by this coming Saturday, a mere three days away. Helen, one of the nursing supervisors and I are sent off to get some pamphlets made. The security office we're sent to don't have any paper. To get paper we have to take a form to the captain for his signature. We meet him in the corridor and follow him down the hall to his office. The room is full of military personnel and *thobed* Arabs milling around with glasses and plates in their hands. It seems we're in the middle of a military *masalamah* (usually a farewell). Next minute Helen and I are sitting on Captain *whatever's* leather chair (didn't catch his name) eating a huge slice of chocolate cake and sipping orange juice. We wait another twenty minutes for the signature then suddenly the power goes off and we're left in total darkness. There is a small commotion while the electricity is switched back on. There is also an absence of air conditioning so we glide our way around the room, retrieve the now signed form and head towards the door. It is stifling hot and there is thunder and lightening. It actually rains for about five seconds. We leave the signed form in Aster's capable hands and leave for home. The roads are strangely quiet. The Saudi's are quite scared of thunder and lightening it turns out. Good for us as we arrive back at least six minutes earlier than usual. I open the apartment door and find Hewa is there. He is sporting a darker head of hair. It's a glossy black actually, but I pretend I don't remember it was nearly gray last week. We go through our routine greeting,

"Hello Madame, and how are you?" Head cocked expectantly to the side.

"I'm fine Hewa. How are you?"

"I am also fine Madame", beaming broadly, "and how is doctor?"

"He's fine Hewa, thank you."

". . . and how is baby?" Tim still cringes when he's called Baby, at seven he quite rightly feels he has the right to be called boy at the very least. Today Hewa offers to read my palm. He takes my hand, turns it over and runs a calloused brown finger ruminatively down the centre of my palm. He looks up and says seriously,

"Madame will live long but," here he pauses dramatically,

"Yes?" I feel a little anxious.

"But Madame will never be rich," he looks down and peers a bit closer at the base of my thumb. I feel hopeful but he shakes his head again sorrowfully,

"No, never rich." He declares firmly. I snatch my hand away slightly irritated. Yeah, I get it. He needn't press the point.

"Well I hope I will have at least enough to pay you today Hewa!" I retort, a little cruelly. A flicker of fear crosses his features but then he laughs,

"Ah Madame is very amusing." he smiles and heads towards the ironing nodding his head.

We decide to see the Hofuf caves which are near Dhahran around an hour and a half away from us. The rocky sandstone area is a beautiful backdrop for the scenery before us. Tom has accompanied us in his 4x4. He tells us that Hofuf is famous for being the largest natural oasis in the world. I gaze slowly around me and see that it is indeed greener than the surrounding area and there are a few more date palms than usual but I see no mirage. We walk up the side of one of the small canyons. It is hot, dusty and tiring but the view from the top is well worth it. Later Tom leads us to a small low-roofed mud building which we enter. An old man in a dusty red stained *thobe* and red and white chequered *ghutra* bends over a primitive pottery wheel, his hands move deftly over the pale clay while his dusty sandal-less feet peddle the wheel as he turns the smooth clay into the beginnings of a thin necked jar. Tim watches him in fascination and he is soon having a go himself under the watchful amused gaze of the potter. He gestures over to one side of the mud floor and we see various pots and vases have been stacked carefully along its length with a few palm leaf woven hats and fans. I buy a few of each as the price is good and I like the simplicity of his design. The clay is unfired so I handle the packages carefully back to the car. There are a number of small thin feral cats around. They all look as though a good meal would not go amiss.

"Let's go and look for the caves. Follow me." says Tom hopping into his land cruiser and slamming the door firmly. We follow him to a large open cave nearby.

"Phew, this place smells!" says Tim wrinkling his nose as he peers around. There are all manner of clothing strewn around the cave in carefree abandon. Well I'm rather hoping it was carefree, the alternative doesn't bear thinking about. There is litter in all corners of the cave, plastic bottles, broken glass, pieces of old leather belt, old tins—mainly 'foul beans' I note, reading one peeling label with interest. These pale beans are very popular with the locals.

We leave Hofuf before 4pm to miss the afternoon traffic.

Here's a quick recipe:

FOUL BEAN DIP

You'll Need:

1 can fava beans
1 lemon, juice of
2 tablespoon olive oil.
1/2 teaspoon salt
1/4 teaspoon pepper
1/4 of a jalapeño

Heat the olive oil in the pan, once hot add chopped clove of garlic. Make sure that garlic is heated on medium for about two minutes. Add Foul beans to pan with juice from the can so that it boils in its own juice along with olive oil and garlic. The beans will boil and absorb the juice. Make sure that they don't dry out. You may also add lemon, garlic, and as much jalapeño as you like. Once the bean concoction has become mushy it's time to serve. serve in a flat bowl. Add salt and lemon to taste.

CHAPTER SIXTEEN

*"When you travel, remember that a
foreign country is not designed to make
you comfortable. It is designed to make
its own people comfortable."*

Clifton Fadiman

Interrogations

TODAY IS THE official opening of the second Fire
exhibition at the nearby college. Lindy and I wait at
Emergency Room (ER) for the hospital transport to
take us there. After an hour June gets up and telephones
Colonel Al-Saftie to find out what the delay is all about.
While she's gone Anna from Personnel comes in and tells

us that Esme, the pretty blonde South African secretary to Colonel Hassan has been in a car accident. Anna tells us she had gone with Ruth and Jenny to a nearby compound with some American man. There had been quite a bit of drinking but he'd insisted on driving and when taking them back to the Corniche centre he went into an oncoming lorry. It hit the side of his car where Esme was sitting. She sustained a broken arm and facial lacerations. The worst thing was that after the police arrived they took blood for alcohol levels from her as well as the American. She had also been over the limit. We are worried what this might mean for her. As the big boss's western secretary and a single woman to boot, it does not look good for her. June returns looking annoyed,

"Can you believe it, we can't go to the exhibition because we're women!" she exclaims flopping down in a plastic seat next to me.

"They could have told us that before we went to all the trouble of making posters and pamphlets." She grumbles. I tell her I'm off to make a card for Esme.

"I'll leave it with her in ICU from all of us." June smiles gratefully, she has a busy ER to get back to. I find Lindy and she accompanies me to see Esme. Victor has already sent her some flowers. Apparently he has also given her a pair of red bloomers. Lindy and I try not to smile. Esme is asleep, her face swollen and bruised. I leave my card next to the bed with some chocolates and a can of juice. Col picks me up later. He had received a call to say a delegation from Riyadh has arrived to look into the case of the 'missing fallopian tube'. I'm cross because he has to drive like the clappers to drop me at home. Wish I could just drive myself.

The full moon has Fayez in a tizz again and he rushes around shouting at everyone. We have a virus on our computer and it is so slow it takes twice as long to get anything typed. Some local has driven into Rehaad's car, which will cost over SR40 000 to repair. Naturally the Saudi won't take the blame as he's a local and Rehaad is Egyptian. It would never have happened if Rehaad wasn't in the country in the first place. He had the cheek to offer to pay SR500! *Snake* is justifiably spitting mad. Grant is writing the first copy of '*The Educator*,' which is to be our first department magazine. Lindy and I have contributed most of the articles. She has embellished our credentials horrifically. I have enough degrees to be walking at right angles. Lindy reasons that they love embellishing things like that here so why shouldn't we. I can think of a few reasons but they don't hold water in the kingdom.

We are going to the Heritage Museum today. It is a low painted mud building outside of Al-Khyber. The two-storey building, with rooms that run off the central hall, houses instruments of war and items of clothing from each of the different provinces. I take a photo of Tim standing with one of the guards, complete with sword. Tim is fascinated. I watched how they prepare proper cardamom coffee and find out that all the guards dressed in Saudi costume are actually Indian! It seems the Saudi work ethic wont even stretch as far as showing off their heritage! We sit downstairs at one of the long wooden tables set for the purpose and have mint tea and *samboosas* before heading back to the compound.

It starts to rain this afternoon and continues till next morning. I can't believe what the place looks like after seven or eight hours of rain. I didn't even know it could rain so much in Saudi. Apparently it doesn't—usually! Peering outside as the taxi drives through a flood of water there are mini lakes everywhere. The water reaches to the doorways of all the shops. I get to work early and step gingerly through puddles of water to the front door. It is locked and everything is in darkness and the electricity is off. There is no one from the department around and no means of entering our office so Lindy and I decide to go off on the bus into town after having breakfast at the cafeteria. Lindy has Len's digital camera with her and she snaps away at all the waterlogged cars and islands of shops in a lake of giant rain puddles. We go to her apartment after shopping and download the photographs onto a floppy disc. Yeah, we are a few years behind CDs at this stage! I take the taxi home at 2pm, it's my turn to be early and Lindy will cover for me. I am home only a few minutes when she calls me. Big problem at work, apparently Dr. H has been looking for her everywhere and then started to look for me as well. He had Rehaad page for us both and even Leanne is involved. Lindy advises me to get back to work *ASAP*. She says Len will be in our area as he was to have picked her up at 2:30. She suggests I get a lift back into the hospital with him. I ask,

"But why were you not at work covering me?" but the line is dead.

Len picks me up and in twenty minutes we approach the main gate. He leans forward and pulls out a handful of plastic coated gate passes and hands me one. I peer at it closely,

"Where did you get this?"

"I made them a few months ago." Replies Len dropping the rest in the glove compartment and shutting the cover firmly.

"It makes it easier for me to drop and fetch Lindy without having to wait in the security line for a card and fill in details every day. They'll get suspicious one day." I peer at the card he has removed,

"What colour is *this* meant to be?" I ask him waving the card under his nose.

"Don't worry," says Len confidently, "It's the yellow card today. I had a look earlier when I dropped Lindy off." I look doubtfully at the photocopied gate pass in my hand.

"Yellow! It looks bile green to me!"

We're still laughing when we stop behind the car in front. The guard is checking his gate pass but for some reason he keeps glancing back at us. I think he's looking at the Bin Laden name on the side of the car. He is suspicious and I have a sinking feeling he's not going to accept the *gate pass*. He doesn't. After Len hands it to him, he glances at me, back to Len and then at the card.

"Come!" He says shortly to Len who climbs out of the car and follows the guard to the small office. I feel sick. Len has made illegal copies of gate passes in a military hospital in Saudi Arabia. He has now been caught. It won't be good. I suddenly remember the rest of the cards and I pull them out of the glove compartment and shove them into my bag. After ten minutes I feel more agitated. It's getting late and Dr. H will still looking for me. Now I am caught in this mess. I get out of the car and enter the office where the guard is questioning Len. I start to babble about being innocent of any wrongdoing and late for work and plead with the guard to let Len drive me to the education department.

"He can come back to explain to you," I beg, tears filling my eyes with ease. I am truly upset. The guard sighs. They hate female emotions at the best of times.

"OK he take you but give first the agama." he holds out his hand and Les hands over his *agama and histamara*. As we drive off towards the office I speak rapidly, telling Len what he should do. He is very pale and I know he is in big trouble. I'm not so sure I'm out of the woods either.

"Look, tell them some local gave you a gate pass. Say you didn't understand what he was doing. Act dumb. Just say he gave you the pass and said you must use it." I shake my head,

"Actually no, don't say he told you anything; he'd be a local. *Mufee englesi*. Say he just gave it to you but didn't say anything." Len nods slowly. His profile looks grim.

"Oh God! There'll be trouble because you gave me a lift."

I cast around for a reason for him to be taking me to work instead of Col as my husband.

"I'll run in and grab a video." I tell a miserable Len as we round the corner to the Education department.

"You tell them that I was at the gate waiting for you. I'd promised to lend you an educational video for your work." Len looks doubtful,

"What would I want to do that for?" I fling open the door,

"I don't bloody know. It doesn't matter, it's just an excuse for you to give the security." I run in breathlessly, bump into Ding who says,

"Ah where *hab* you been? Dr. Al-Hammad look for you all day." I rush past him ignoring his bewildered face and grab a video from my table. I glance at the title, '*CPR for beginners*' it would have to do.

"Here!" I thrust the cassette through the window at Len.

"Tell them I brought this to you at the gate and you felt bad having me walk back in the heat so you offered to drive me to the office. Say you were given the gate pass while waiting in line so you decided to use it to save time." I babble breathlessly. Len smiles grimly,

"I hope this will work." I wish him luck and rush back inside to face the music of a different tune. I start by looking for Lindy. Every place I try. I'm met with a shrug.

"I heard them looking for you two." says Sanette as I rush past Post Partum.

"Yeah, we were busy in Outpatients." I mutter. I can't find Lindy anywhere so I walk back to the Education department, trying to avoid anyone who may feel the need to tell me, 'Everyone's looking for you.' I bump into Aziz and he asks me where have I been all day.

"I can account for my day." I tell him angrily, knowing he is fully aware that Lindy and I were at the Corniche earlier. Lindy and Dr. H arrive at the same time. Dr. Hammad asks how I am and how is Tim and Colin. I stammer that we are all well. Lindy winks at me so I assume she has given him some story. I say I am busy with lectures and he leaves us for prayers. Lindy hears my story and is open-mouthed when I tell her Len has been caught and is still at the Security gate being questioned. At that minute the phone rings. It is Len. He tells me they still have him answering questions.

"Have you given them the story we discussed?" I ask nervously.

"Yes, but they don't believe me. They keep asking where I got the fake gate pass and how come you came with me." I feel cold. Poor Len. He sounds tired.

"Never mind," I say with as much confidence as I can muster,

"Hang in there. There are only so many times they can ask you the same questions. Just keep telling them the same thing." He asks after Lindy and I feel irritated that he's worrying about *her* in the circumstances,

"Don't worry about Lindy. Col will give her a lift when he collects me. Worry about yourself and getting out of this as quickly as possible." I replace the receiver slowly and turn to Lindy who has been listening.

"Don't worry," I repeat, "I'll ask Col to drop you off at the Gulf. I'm just so worried about Len "I tell her sinking into my chair. Lindy nods,

"What a day!" She tells me she'd given Dr. H some sob story about having a *'woman's problem'* that had necessitated me accompanying her back to the Corniche. I tell her it was a good excuse as he wouldn't be able to bring himself to discuss such an intimate detail with a woman. When Col comes to collect us, I fill him in with the turn of events.

"Let's go to the gate office and see how Len is doing," I plead. Len is still in the same chair looking exhausted. Col speaks to the guard and tells him that he is my husband and Len a friend of his,

"I give him permission to take my wife," says Col firmly. The guard looks non-committal and asks for my *agama* and hospital ID. He makes a photocopy of it and hands it back wordlessly. Len tells me quickly that he has given the same story as I'd earlier suggested. He leans forward slightly and whispers,

"Lindy must not be implicated at all," looking at me earnestly,

"She would lose her job if they knew I was fetching her every day. They think you are my girlfriend." I look at him incredulously,

"Well I hope you told them I'm no such thing!" Len glances quickly at the guards who are discussing the case in Arabic.

"Look it will be OK for you. You have Colin. She has no one. I have to stay and wait for some general or other to arrive. Don't worry just don't mention Lindy."

We are allowed to leave and we join Lindy who is sitting in the car waiting for us.

"What's happening?" She asks. I slam the car door,

"He's in there protecting you at all costs," I reply, fear making me angry.

"I hope you appreciate how much he does for you."

"Of course I do!" Lindy looks both anxious and relieved.

Col and I drive back in silence after dropping her off. We discuss the situation and decide as long as he keeps to his story; it should all blow over by the evening. It doesn't! Colin is worried how my presence will be implicated in the situation and what it may mean for my job and even staying in Saudi. I phone Len at around 10:30 to find out what is happening. He is still being questioned. He has been moved to another office. He tells me that he is sticking to his story but says they are asking more questions now about me.

I doze off around 12 but phone Len again at 4:30 am. He is still there but is being allowed to leave at 5am.

"I must return at 12 tomorrow, or rather later today." I picture him glancing at his watch. He sounds utterly exhausted and says he has never felt more tired. Col is angry with both Len and Lindy this morning,

"Why couldn't they just come clean and tell the truth!" he says as he drives me to work. I look at him,

"The truth about the gate card?" Col shakes his head,

"No, I mean about his involvement with Lindy, that the reason he made so many false gate passes is so that he can take her in and out of the hospital. You were just unlucky to get caught with him. It should have been Lindy!"

I stare ahead and wonder how my day is going to go. I'm tired but Len will be exhausted. I hope he's managed to get some sleep.

Dr. Al-Hammad calls me into his office. He closes the door behind him and sits down,

"What has happened to you yesterday?" He asks stroking his moustache with one finger. I feel tears pricking my eyelids and I tell him the same story as Len has been telling the security staff since 2:30 yesterday afternoon. Dr. H looks at me for a moment then says quietly,

"He must be a very bad man," he raises his hand to shush me as I vehemently rise to defend Len's honour.

"You must go to see Colonel Azeer at 9 O'clock in the security building". Azeer is chief of security and I feel a shiver of dread and foreboding. Dr. H accompanies me to the security office and chats quickly with Al-Azeer then leaves. I am asked to sit down in a leather chair and he asks me several questions.

"Why were you with Mr. Carraway in his car yesterday afternoon?"

I answer him as clearly as possible but the story sounds implausible even to my ears.

"He needed an educational video for his work to train staff in CPR," I begin nervously,

"So I took it to the Gate to drop it off for him. When he arrives to collect it, he wanted to take me back to my office because it was too hot to walk." I finish lamely.

"Why did he not wait in the line for the security gate pass?" he asks me sternly. A good bloody question! Why didn't he!

"Because I was late and someone had given him the fake pass," he stares at me and then scribbles something down on a pad. Eventually he gets up and leaves the office for a while. I look around his sparse office gazing vacantly at the certificates in Arabic along the wall, the leather accessories adorning his huge walnut table complete with the usual carved name plaque. He returns,

"Come! You will go to the security police department. It is close to the hospital." I stand up feeling cold and nervous. The police! Oh God no! What have I got myself into? He leads me to a sinister looking black Mercedes with tinted windows parked outside and ushers me into the back seat. I find myself seated next to a thin local in a white *thobe* and chequered head cloth. He is smoking a cigarette. He places the cigarette in his mouth and offers his hand, which I take nervously, not knowing what to expect,

"I am Joe. I will be your translator." He has a kind face and speaks with a slight American accent.

"Th.thank you." I stammer. We drive in silence until we reach what must be police head quarters, a low gray building with barbed wire along the walls. I am led into a room in which four other Saudi military personnel are seated. They barely look up as Joe ushers me in. Perching on a hard metal chair I look around nervously. The man behind the desk is in full military regalia.

"This is the chief of military secret police." Joe informs me leaning forward in his armchair and whispering quietly while puffing on his cigarette. I nod uncertainly and wait. The three military men chat among themselves in Arabic ignoring me and I feel very uncomfortable. Eventually one of the men leaves the room and the interrogation begins. The man behind the desk asks me questions in Arabic. Joe translates and I answer. He translates my answers back to the general who remains grim faced throughout the ordeal.

"What is your relationship to Mr. Leonard Carraway?" he begins. Wow! No gentle introduction here! I say he is a friend of my husbands, stressing the word 'husband'. How long have I known him, how often do we meet. Does my husband approve of our relationship, are some of the questions they ask. At first it is merely a case of answering and waiting for the translation but as the hours roll by the questions become more complex as though they are trying to trap me. I try and maintain my composure. I instinctively know they will not take kindly to feminine wiles such as tears and pleading. I answer in short emphatic sentences and bring in Col's name as often as I can. They continuously accuse me of being Lens's girlfriend. I am emphatic in my denial and say Col would be very angry to hear that. My chair is hard and uncomfortable. They take turns in questioning. I'm thirsty but am not offered anything to drink and I'm not going to ask. People come and go leaving me alone, even Joe has to leave for lunch and the loo I reason. I produce the video that I inform them I had wanted to lend Len, that being the reason for the lift and nothing more. They don't react and merely continue with the questioning,

"When did you and Mr. Carraway decide to make your own gate passes?"

"How often do you leave the hospital to meet Mr. Carraway?"

"How many people are involved in this?"

"Have I ever provided any military information to Mr. Carraway?"

"How long has Mr. Carraway worked for Bin Laden?"

The questions continue, becoming more bizarre until I feel like weeping in frustration. I haven't slept more than two hours all night and do not feel I can keep this up for much longer. The hours pass. At around 12:30. There is a break and without telling me anything, my translator leaves the room again with the others and I am left alone for about forty minutes. I wonder whether they've locked the door and even contemplate making a run for it. Around 1:15 two men return. They sit and light up cigarettes and presumably discuss the case. I wriggle uncomfortably in my seat. My bottom has long since gone numb and my bladder is filling up rapidly.

My stomach gurgles accusingly. I had a small bowl of porridge at 7 this morning and my tongue is dry. When Joe returns I jump up and tell him I desperately need the loo. He translates rapidly and a guard leads me outside to a toilet. It smells strongly of urine and there are puddles all over the floor. I wipe the seat down carefully before taking a seat. My hands tremble as I wash them under a trickle of water and I wonder what the outcome of this sorry business will be. I am wondering how Len is faring. Earlier Joe had whispered that he is in another part of the building also being interrogated. They will compare our answers he says lighting up yet another cigarette. The interrogation continues, questions coming thick and fast. I fall over my answers but manage not to implicate Lindy at any time, even when they ask me if Len has given me a lift before. I don't know what he has told them. I have in fact had many lifts from Len but always with Lindy sitting in the front. Maybe the guards know this and have informed the police who will know if I lie. But then they would also know that it is Lindy who Len comes to visit and all the questioning so far has been regarding our relationship. I decide to say I have received a lift before but with my husband's permission. They debate my answer a while. I glance quickly at my watch. It is now 3:20. I have been here for over six hours. I am so tired I could curl up on the floor and sleep but still the same questions continue, I give the same answers but now they are trying a different angle,

"Mr. Carraway tells us you made the gate passes for him so that he could visit you in the hospital," they tell me. I shake my head emphatically,

"No, no that's not true. Len has *never* visited *me.*" I give the word the slightest inflection but it is lost in translation. On and on it goes till I feel like screaming. At one point I wonder how on earth Len managed to stay sane after more than 12 hours.

Suddenly at 4:15 it's all over. I am asked to sign some document written in Arabic. I take the form and look at Joe with raised eyebrows. He nods so I sign it and then I am released and taken back to the education department. I do not know what their decision is as they haven't bothered to tell me but at this stage I am just grateful to be released from the torture. I alight from the back of the shiny black car with weak knees and walk into the office to phone Col. Lindy enters the office while I am talking to him. When I put down the phone she asks me if I told them anything about her. I am furious,

"No Lindy, I did not tell them anything about *you,*" I reply coldly.

"Your reputation remains intact." I grab my bag and head for the door. Her eyes fill with tears,

"You don't understand," she says dabbing at her eyes,

"They'll deport me if they found out I was seeing Len; I would lose my job and everything. Jerry and the family are depending on me." I look at her as I open the office door,

"Yes I know." I say quietly, "and I could lose mine!" I slam the door and go and sit outside for a minute. Rehaad finds me sitting on the steps and says Captain Azeer wants to see me again. With heavy heart I trudge slowly down to his office, knock on the door and enter. He doesn't look up from writing and I stand uncomfortably for a few minutes with my arms behind my back, army style until he looks up.

"You must write a statement" he says handing me a document. I don't understand,

"I thought I had sir?" He looks down at his desk again and speaks coldly,

"You must write again everything you did yesterday when you were caught with Mr. Carraway." I nod and walk over to a chair to start scribbling. Yesterday! Was it only yesterday the whole nightmare began? While I am writing Azeer suddenly asks me,

"Why did you take a taxi to the gate?" I look up at him, bugger, I'd forgotten about that,

"I wanted to get to the gate quickly so I could give my husband's friend Leonard a video tape." I repeat the story for the hundredth time. He sighs heavily before asking,

"Why did he not get a gate pass and come to fetch the video himself?" his cold eyes bore into me. My mind races, yes, why didn't he, what should I say?

"He was in a hurry and didn't want to wait." Azeer looks at me a moment, long brown fingers fiddling with his pen.

"It does not make sense then to still offer to take you back." He states. I'm scared and a little irritated, this is yet another interrogation. I am tired and just want to go home and lie down and sleep. I don't answer him but finish off my statement and hand it back to him.

"Thank you sir." I say as firmly as possible, "Will that be all?" He glances down at the document I've just handed him as though debating whether to let me go or not.

"Dr. Al-Hammad speaks highly of your work," he says shortly,

"Be more careful in future." I back out of his office,

"I will sir, thank you very much." I leave quickly before he thinks of something else to ask me, and head back to the department. I phone Len and he tells me he has also been let go with a severe warning. He is not to return to the Hospital ever again. I momentarily wonder how Lindy is going to manage without her consort to fetch and carry her. I tell him he is very lucky.

"I took a friend from work," Len tells me, "I think that must have helped." I tell him to go home and sleep.

"They asked me if I'd ever given you a lift before." says Len,

"I'm glad you told me to say no because my first instinct was to say I had." I agree it was fortuitous we'd spoken about this and decide not to tell him I had told the truth. We plan to meet up at the hash camp tomorrow.

I tell Col everything that happened today. He looks livid but merely tells me to have a bath and go to sleep.

CHAPTER SEVENTEEN

"Do not follow where the path may lead. Go instead where there is no path and leave a trail"

Ralph Waldo Emerson

Christmas Dinner

WE HEAR THAT Sue has cancelled the hash camp due to impending rain but we all decide to meet up anyway. The day is pleasantly cool with a light breeze and the clouds are a steel gray in the distance. We meet up with Len, Lindy, Ruth and Jenny, the two physiotherapists from South Africa at the large dune 10km outside town. We drive on a bit further to the same spot we had stayed at last year and set up camp near a large sandy overhang of sandstone. As we are sitting in a small semi circle enjoying an early nightcap, a blue 4X4 draws up and a long faced man with dark hair peers out at us,

"Is this the Al-Khyber hash camp?" he enquires. We nod and he pulls over and hops out,

"Hi I'm Chris, we're from the Jubail hash group." he nods over at a large overweight man who has jumped out of the passenger side,

"He's Chuck." Chris and Chuck are from Canada. Chuck wears a waistcoat and a black Stetson on his head. They ask to join our group and we happily oblige—the more the merrier. We decide to do a spot of rock climbing over the rocky sandstone ridge, which is glowing pinkly in the setting sun. It remains cool but the rain holds off. Ruth becomes a hunter-gatherer and collects dead wood and twigs for the campfire. I collect interesting offerings for the fire such as dried camel dung and tufts of dried grass. The flames takes them hungrily and we are soon sitting around a small but effective fire sipping more home brew courtesy of Len who, after yesterday must need it as much as I do!

"Why was the camp cancelled?" Asks Chris in his heavy Canadian accent. I point up at the clear starry night sky,

"Because of the rain!" everyone laughs.

We BBQ some meat and chat till around 11 when it suddenly becomes freezing, as it does in the desert. Tim and Lindy are sharing a tent leaving Len to fold himself somewhat miserably into the Toyota. We wake early this morning. The sky is streaked pink and mauve and there is a chill in the air. I grab my wash bag and head for the nearest dune. After a basic breakfast of tea and tinned fruit salad we set off for a short walk. The Canadians leave after breakfast and head back to Jubail. We come across a small caravan of camels led by a Pakistani *Bedouin*. Ruth asks him if we can have a ride on one of the camels which he agrees to for a small sum. He leads a pale camel towards us. Tim and Ruth are brave enough to have a go first then the evil-smelling thing is led to me. He has green stuff coming out of his nether regions and green froth out of the other and I suppress a heave as the tattered rope lead is handed over to me. He is flea bitten and mangy and I grab at the rough course hair of his back as he kneels in front of me in the sand on calloused knees. It is a very strange sensation climbing onto a camel, as you cling on, it moves forward to get up and you feel as though you will be thrown over its head and then it stands up and suddenly it tilts backwards and you are convinced you will fall off. The hair around his middle is strangely soft and warm against my legs and he plods around slowly led by his Pakistani owner. Ruth takes a few photos then the forward backward movement occurs again in reverse.

"That was weird!" says Tim eyes shining with pleasure at the weirdness of it.

The saga of the military display continues and we are told we need to prepare again. I run around getting more pamphlets and posters made. We are driven to the exhibition hall by the hospital bus and meet Al-Saftie who is still wearing his blue 'fire and safety' overalls and running around ineffectually. We hear that the exhibition is for men only.

"Not again!" I exclaim irritably, "How come they only manage to discover this after we've done all the work!" We drop off the pamphlets and similar paraphernalia and are driven back to the hospital. Doctor H calls me to his office, hands me a small juice can and asks me how Len is. I shrug,

"I haven't seen him since last week." I lie, having seen him the day before. Dr. Hammad stares at me for a few seconds before saying darkly that I must be careful because,

"They are watching you!" Great. Now I'm a hardened criminal watched by the Saudi military police. Are they watching Lindy I wonder before asking him if I may leave early, as Tim is home alone with a raging bout of tonsillitis. He can't even make this decision himself and begins waffling about having been squeezed about managing his staff. I go and ask Aziz who I know has a young daughter. He says I can go and I take a taxi back to KWMH. Poor Tim is burning with fever. It is after a month like this one, where Tim has to be left alone so much that I can't bear the thought of spending another year in Saudi.

Al-Hammad is in a puff this morning because he's heard Aziz is leaving. He adds, somewhat cryptically, that he doesn't want the military taking over as 'we' would not like it. More likely HE won't like being found out that he spends half his time away in the land of *infidels* methinks! Aziz lends an air of consistency to the department. He can make a decision all by himself unlike Dr. Hammad. Unfortunately he is due to retire. Dr. H has come to rely on him more and more since he joined the department a little over a year ago.

It is Ramadan and we have to sneak around at meal times and hide the kettle in the office for our tea. Everyone is in a bad mood. We tiptoe around as quietly as we can and pray for the end of Ramadan. Lindy brings me a packet from Len who has returned from Bahrain. It has a huge cheddar cheese and some ham, carefully wrapped up in white paper. I'm always happy to get some good cheddar and of course ham is always welcome. These days Len drops Lindy outside the main gate and she either walks or thumbs a lift to the department. During prayer time at Ramadan I am tip-toeing past Mr. Aziz's office with a glass of water when I peer in and I nearly drop my glass. He is sitting back in his easy chair, smoking, drinking coffee and reading a newspaper!

Col meets me in the hospital, as he needs to speak with Dr. Muhktar again about our plan to take leave in India. As we are striding down the corridor with military staff all around arguing mildly Col suddenly stops and says he feels hypo and shaky. Without thinking I reach into the packet Len gave me and tear off a huge chunk of cheddar and thrust it into Col's mouth. Col hisses,

"It's Ramadan you idiot, what am I supposed to do with this?"

He hauls the cheese out of his mouth and shoves it quickly into his pocket but this hasn't gone unnoticed. We rush to the next corner laughing. Col shoves the lint-covered cheese back into his mouth. What a business. It seems so unnatural. Last week I had taken my morning cup of coffee into lectures and had sipped away merrily for half an hour between talking when suddenly I had realized my *faux pas*. Half the Orientees are Moslem from Thailand and are presently fasting. I had felt terrible and apologized profusely then spent the next hour feeling irritated that I had to apologize, feeling it is their custom that caused the embarrassment in the first place!

Dr. H arrives at 11am and calls us both Lindy and I to the office. He says he is delighted to hear we have cancelled a lecture to be at his meeting, which just goes to show he hasn't a clue. As we're returning to our office we hear the overhead pager calling urgently for, 'O Positive' blood donors. Lindy looks at me and says,

"Let's go!" and before I have time to think, we're marching down the long corridor towards the blood bank.

A Filipina 'phlebotomist' takes us to the back room and asks us to sit in one of three narrow beds. She takes a prick of blood to check our haemaglobin levels. Mine is OK at 13mg% but Lindy's is only 10.6mg%, which is too low to give blood. Lindy being Lindy however, corners the doctor sitting in front and he eventually agrees that she may donate, provided she only gives 350mls of blood. We are asked to lie down and two white-coated Filipina phlebotomists try to find a suitable vein, using their bare hands. Gloves are usually mandatory in any country but Saudi. It's funny that, when they are so particular about HIV/AIDS. They appear to be teaching a third Filipina what to do and the air is thick with *Tagalog*. Along with the absence of gloves is the absence of information. They shove a needle into my vein without warning and leave me draining my lifeblood away. I feel nervous as this is my first time to donate blood and I do feel guilty that we are to be paid for it. Lindy is fine, having done this many times before but I begin to feel cold and dizzy so she asks them to bring me a juice, which I drink gratefully. We are paid SR500 in cash and leave for the department clutching another juice. I feel slightly strange all day, disoriented and weak. Can't understand why, especially when I look at Lindy who is practically bloodless by now. She is rushing up and down with seemingly boundless energy. I suspect my feelings are probably more psychological in origin. I like my blood to remain in my body generally. Then I think of my pint saving a life and feel better.

Col takes me to Giant stores after work, to look for some yellow tights for Tim's school play. Giant stores, as the name implies, sells huge industrial sizes of produce. I know I'll be able to get some tights there. Tim is to play the head of the skylark formation. I can only find a pair in beige. I end up dying them at home with a bottle of food colouring, which stains everything but the damn tights!

Lindy has found a policy that says we are entitled to three days off for having donated blood. She tries to get her three days tagged onto her leave but Dr. H is having none of it. She has to take the days before her leave. We hear that there has been another bomb blast in Khyber. A British man got his eyes and hands burned, this is worrying and I feel anxious that it occurred close to Tim's school. This type of activity is becoming more common and is starting to make us uneasy.

I am up early this morning to prepare for Christmas dinner. We owe quite a few people a meal so I have invited them all for Christmas supper tonight. I spend a few hours tidying and polishing and moving furniture around. Quiches and salads, rice, chicken pate, are on the menu. Last but not least I take out a HUGE turkey from the fridge and unwrap the outer plastic covering. I bought it last night at Giant stores because it says on the label that there is a *red popper*, which you must depress before cooking, and when it's ready the red popper does just that—it pops out (apparently fool proof.) I buy two large red and white striped Saudi stuffed cushions at the local petrol station to add colour and help distract from the drab browns. Henry sold me some beer and wine and I have a couple bottles of my own red. I shove the turkey in the oven at around 5pm. It is so big it only just fits and it is still in situ when everyone arrives at 7:15. I have had a five-minute shower and dressed in a white skirt and top. I'm feeling exhausted but try not to show it as Jean and Chaz arrive. Jean presents me with a lovely poinsettia plant, which goes very nicely with the cushions. Mahe and Rojish arrive with a plastic bottle of red, Tom and Anthony ditto. I seat everyone around the lounge and hiss at Col to give them a drink while I go I to check the turkey. I open the oven door and peer in, nearly singeing my eyebrows in the process. The popper still hasn't popped but it is ½ an hour over the cooking time so I remove the tray carefully and set it down on the counter. I suddenly notice small black bits of something unidentifiable swimming around the turkey juice.

"I wonder what it is?" I peer closer whilst stirring the gravy into the juices in the pan and reveal a naked knife blade. It appears I have cooked a kitchen knife with the turkey which I note with some dismay is so well cooked, the meat is literally falling off the bone—in dry lumps! I try and pick out bits of plastic from the gravy but give up when I smell burning. The peas have dried to wrinkled hard balls and I'm turning round to find a place to put the pan when I hear my name, I swing round and the pan slips from my hand, releasing hundreds of little hard pea balls to the floor where they roll around as if trying to escape.

"Can I help you with anything?" Jean stands poised in the doorway with a bewildered look on her face as I fix a frozen and unconvincing smile on my face,

"No, no Jean, thanks really. It's fine. I'll be there in a mo." Jean does not look convinced but she retreats with a smile. She's no sooner out of the room and I'm on my knees picking up as many peas as I can off the floor. I fling them into a glass bowel and run some cold water over them. I have to microwave the peas to heat them up again which hardens them even more. The gravy has started to congeal unappetizingly around the leathery turkey pieces and the rice is also starting to burn. I plonk the lot on a tray and bring it through to the table. Everyone is chatting animatedly and I hope they won't notice the meal is a total disaster. I go around filling everyone's glasses to make sure they don't!

"Dinner is ready." I trill above the sound of chatter and laughter. I swing round and knock a bottle of red onto the starched white linen tablecloth that Hewa had so lovingly ironed. The stain spreads quickly despite my furious mopping.

"Hey, that's my wine!" exclaims Col.

"I know, but I heard you must remove red wine stains with white."

It's not working though, so I have to remove every item from the tablecloth in order to remove the unsightly cloth. Several guests murmur that it doesn't matter but I'm determined. I have no more tablecloths so a white bed sheet has to do. I notice that there is not enough cutlery on the table. We only have the standard number of six of everything. I gulp down a glass of red and fumble in the kitchen drawer for any available implement. I find three more forks, one with only two prongs and five teaspoons. These will have to be for Col, Tim and I. Everyone is seated around the table and valiantly tucking into hard dry slivers of turkey, burnt rice, cold quiche (I did not have enough room in the oven to heat it), bullet peas, oh and congealed gravy with sautéed kitchen knife. I notice with horror that at least three people are picking bits of black plastic out of their mouths. Mahe has shot a dozen hard peas from her spoon across the table. I turn up the music to drown out the sounds of valiant munching.

"So how long does it take for a turkey to cook?" asks Anthony removing a pea from his wine glass.

"You have to wait for the red popper to pop." I answer enigmatically and get up to remove the plates of disastrous Christmas fare. I ask Colin to please refill the glasses and head for the kitchen. I lean against the kitchen counter and press a cold cloth against my cheeks. The jug of congealing gravy topples off the counter as I turn to open the fridge, and I have to wipe up gravy off the floor with a kitchen towel. Dessert is ice cream and Christmas pudding, which I plate up using a basting knife as we've run out of cutlery. I set the bowl down with a flourish and dish up for everyone. Tom is sitting in a chair in the corner chatting to Col. I advance with a bowl of Christmas pudding and ice cream,

"Would you like some pud. Tom?" He doesn't have time to answer because the bowl leaves my still-greasy hands as I'm approaching and in slow motion the following scene unfolds; he sees the bowl descending rapidly towards his lap and simultaneously turns in the chair to avoid full impact while grabbing hold of the waistband of my skirt for support, this in turn draws the skirt rapidly downwards and reveals my panties and gravy stained thighs to the assembled audience. For a few seconds there is a stunned silence as everyone stares first at Tom with the bowl of ice cream seeping unbecomingly into his crotch, to the sight of me with my skirt round my thighs. My mouth forms a perfect 'O'. The silence is deafening then suddenly someone laughs. This sets off some one else and in a few seconds more everyone is howling with laughter while I alternately drag my skirt back to my middle and dab ineffectually at Tom's groin with a cushion, while pouring out apologies with each dab.

"Well now that the entertainment is over, I need a drink!" I mumble to the hysterical audience and flee for the bedroom. Col has to coax me out five minutes later saying everyone has really enjoyed the meal and he's starting to show our slides from our India holiday. Everyone is indeed very polite and when they leave a few hours later they say they've enjoyed the show! I find hard peas for days afterwards under the chairs, settee and table.

Christmas day in Saudi Arabia is like any other day—except worse! I am up early so that Tim can open his presents and we can spend a bit of time with him. We give him his huge life-size stuffed white tiger (which Darlene bought for us in Bahrain), a game-boy (thanks Whiplash!) and several books. He is delighted with his gifts and Col and I sit watching him while we sip our morning tea. But then it's time to get ready for work.

At the hospital, I do my walkabout so everyone can see I'm on duty. Chat to Amelia and Sue, who is in a bad mood because she was on supervisor duty and missed a good Christmas party. She tells me that one of the VIP's had wanted a complete change of furniture! Jenny tells me about being called out for X-rays for an 'urgent' case involving a young boy who was apparently unable to walk. He was however miraculously able to climb from the trolley to the X-ray table when she got there. Dr. *Who* wishes me a happy Christmas which I thought sweet of him. He says I can go, so happily I phone for a taxi. At home I phone mum who is at Jo's house for Christmas. I speak with the rest of the family; John, Jo, Sean, Vi, Jacqui and Daniel and wish them all a happy Christmas. Nanny has apparently gone home to sort out Percy the dog, who has eaten the cactus! It is nice speaking with them and it feels strange to be spending the day in an Islamic country rather than with them.

Today is officially the start of Eid as someone; somewhere significant has spotted a sliver of a new moon. The atmosphere at work is so much better. Everyone in high spirits wishing each other a happy *Eid Mubarak* and exchanging gifts and kisses in equal quantity (specially the males for some reason) Boxes of chocolates are sent round to each department. I leave at 1pm and get ready at home for our trip to Wadi Howtah; a seven hour journey south-west of Riyadh in the central province. There are two routes from Riyadh both on tarmac apart from the last five Kilometres. The journey down Wadi Howtah is very pretty. The villages are old and photogenic. We pack up the land cruiser as quickly as we can and set off. Anthony Carson and Tom Roberts join us. I am tired after the early start and morning at work but look forward to a spot of relaxation in the desert. Having stopped in one of the small towns for petrol, I am able to buy some more milk at the small kiosk attached to the station and we arrive at Daphna sands at around seven and decide to camp there for the night. It was 9pm by the time we had the tent up. We sit around in with all the vehicles positioned in a semi-circle *laager,* sipping home made wine and chatting to Tom and Anthony until around 10pm. I wake up some time in the middle of the night because I am freezing. As I struggle to find warmth under my blanket, I feel Tim next to me. He is frozen solid! I shake him but he's unresponsive. I panic and start to wrap him up in anything I can find in the dark tent, including Col's sleeping bag,

"Col, wake up! Tim has frozen like an ice lolly!" Col leans over me and sees Tim is very pale but suddenly he stirs and I whisper, "Thank God" and cuddle up to him. I too am freezing despite wearing two jerseys and two vests and I can't go back to sleep for a while.

This morning Col photographs me emerging from the tent; bad tempered, frazzled with a bush of hair and crumpled clothes. I am not amused and snarl at him to make me some tea. We don't have much time after this before we are on our way again. We are to meet up with Jean and Chaz at the Wadi reserve. The sandstone cliffs are beautiful in the early morning sun. It is very dry but there are some acacias and a thick, green leafed tree, which also has a purple flower and round fruit pods. We set up camp in the dry *wadi* bed. A *wadi* generally refers to a valley or dry riverbed, which may fill with water following a lot of rain. A group of Americans have made camp close by. The others take a short walk while I unpack and then I have a twenty-minute nap. Later in the afternoon we go for a drive around the area. We see a few *Idmi*, a type of Arabian gazelle, which are listed as vulnerable. Once widespread all over the Arabian Peninsula, the *Idmi* is now declining due to illegal hunting and live capture. They look a bit like springbok. We see them along the edge of the sandstone mountain. They are very skittish and don't hang around for long. Not surprising when you consider the amount of hunting that goes on in Saudi. We find a natural spring high in the sandstone gulley with palm trees and a square pool reminiscent of Lady Anne's bath in Kirstenbosch, Cape Town back home. There are some things of interest on the way back, such as pigeon roosts high up in tall cylindrical shapes, a Toyota with a black and a white camel in the back, huge Subaru's with a number of veiled women in the back, ice-cream coloured garages complete with mosque and a shop painted lime and pink. We find a sinkhole near Howdah. A hole in the fence near the entrance allows us to enter and climb through to join a throng of locals who are circumnavigating slowly around the hole, much as they do in Mecca. We peer carefully into the abyss and see the glimmer of water at the bottom. My disheveled appearance causes a slight stir with my jeans, boots and short T-shirt visible beneath my loosely flowing *abaya*. I had flung it on just before we stopped. The wind blows warmly onto our faces now it is midday. We head back to the car and set off. There are many more scenes of interest. Groups of men in prayer are dotted around the dunes as ' we drive by. Small groups of veiled women bow towards Mecca, white *thobed* men kneel towards the West, small family groups sitting on frayed but opulent carpets in rich blues and reds eating at the roadside. I muse that it is a pity that authentic Bedouin culture is lacking these days.

Corrugated roofs and tin have replaced black tents which were once made from hand spun or woven goat hair. Camels and sheep are transported around the popular Toyota open back truck; satellite aerials have replaced story time around the fire.

We have the first *check point Charlie* near Daphna dunes.

"*Eid mubarack.*" I greet the uniformed guard. He peers through the window at me and notes everything is in order (i.e. I am suitably covered and my seatbelt is in place) so everything is '*kwaeesh, maalish* (fine) which is always better than a big *mushkila (problem).* We stop later on to photograph a small caravan of camels against a red dune backdrop. A baby camel suckles against its mother's warm belly. Some (genuine) Bedu arrive and chat with us while we photograph the camels. We smile and nod and they smile broadly which pretty much sums up the conversation. As we continue along the black snake of tarmac I note the many vehicle 'carcasses' that dot the landscape. Accidents are merely pushed into the surrounding dunes where they remain until the rusty remains are buried in the sand.

After seeing in the New Year with a few glasses of red I'm a little late in to work the following day, and I creep in via the back way. Needn't have bothered! No one is in except *Biktor*, Ding and Astor. Victor gives me a big wet slobbery kiss. He's getting altogether far too familiar since Lindy left on vacation. He hands me some Filipino sweetmeats and stands grinning owl-like in his black-rimmed specs. I peer into the glass at the gelatinous rice concoction and smile weakly. He tells me later that the Filipino tradition, shared with the Chinese, is to set out twelve round fruits on a table before the New Year for good luck. I show my amazement and ask if he has done this yet. June arrives at ER bleary-eyed having come in at 6am from a New Year's party. I make her a strong mug of coffee. She tells me she had been called out to see one of the princesses yesterday while on duty. The guard tells her the princess has a temperature and needs medication. June arrives and notes that she is already on antibiotics and her temperature is a healthy 37, 2 ° C. Both her pulse and blood pressure are text book normal. June had to fuss around her a bit and when she left, the princess was suddenly feeling much better. Last year, she tells me, the base commander had called for someone to come to his house. He had insisted on a 'blonde' Westerner! She had tried to get out of it by saying her husband was expecting her and next minute she was being called by the Programme Director himself who insisted *she* go! Sometimes it is actually good to have red hair in Saudi!

This afternoon Col and I almost come to blows over who is turning into a *camel*, him or me. I reckon he and Tim's manner of letting me carry all the shopping in the heat dressed in black from head to toe while they stroll five paces ahead of me is definitely a contestant for *camelisation*. His only comeback is that I am starting to bargain with everyone for a lower price. Yes, I think I won that round!

I'm visiting the *Royal Saudi Airforce Show and exhibit*, which is being held at the old Dhahran airport hangar. I take my video camera along. The exhibits are surprisingly good. I have plenty of opportunity to videotape the general atmosphere and the many Saudi families arriving in their droves to have a look at the planes and exhibits. Victor also arrives with his camera. He quite fancies himself as a professional and struts around taking studied photos of anything he likes including a wilting flower display against a military water canister! There are parachutists and air displays, helicopters in formation and examples of military aircraft. Colin and Tim join me later and we all have another look before driving home.

CHAPTER EIGHTEEN

"Like all great travelers, I have seen more than I remember, and remember more than I have seen."

Benjamin Disraeli

The End

Today is 'Red letter' day or should I say red 'email' day! Col receives a job offer he can't refuse from a large pathology laboratory in Cape Town. I have to resign in three months! I am in a daze all day. I type out a letter of resignation and hand it to Rehaad the next morning. Ding is in the office when he opens it. There is stunned silence when he reads the contents,

"*Shjaanette,* is this true?" he asks, waving my letter around. I nod excitedly but it looks like they don't share my joy, which is rather touching.

"I weel have to inform Dr Al-Hammad immediately"

"I had to resign, Rehaad," I tell him earnestly, "my husband has another job. You understand that I have to do whatever my husband tells me. I have to go wherever he goes."

This is naturally not strictly true but I feel a glimmer of satisfaction that I have used their own cultural principles to make a subtle point.

Grant Rea returns from his short leave in the Philippines today. He also has a job offer he will take later this year. He gives me a present from Philippines; some dried banana with caramel, white chewy sweets and a necklace and bracelet made from shells. It is so sweet of him. I'll miss his round happy face. Victor is miserable. He hands me a fake flower for my hair and says he's very sorry I'm leaving.

"Never mind," I say briskly, "Lindy is coming back soon." I'm almost upset when his eyes light up. Ah well easy come, easy go! Dr. Al-Hammad is very quiet when he hears of my resignation and says if I change my mind he would be happy. I'm quite fond of the bugger really and only just resist hugging his sagging shoulders. We have a newcomer to the department today as well. I am introduced to Joe and straight away recognize my interpreter during the '*Lengate*' affair. He is much more relaxed when not interrogating! He jokes a lot and when Grant asks him if his wife is veiled he replies,

"Heck no! Why would I want her to look like a ninja?" I am quite amused at his irreverence. Victor leans over my desk this morning and tells me apropos of nothing that he used to dissect '*progs*' back in the *Philippines*. I murmur a suitable response and manage not to smile.

I have the depressive taxi driver again this morning. He sighs with such deep sorrow; I'm scared he's going to fling himself out of the taxi one day, leaving me to drive from the back.

This evening we are introduced to our first Saudi truffle. Chas and Jean have invited us for supper and Jean has outdone herself again. We have mackerel pie with a delicious cheesy short crust pastry, potatoes that are floury and a delicate garlic sauce. The piece de resistance,—truffles. The *zubaidi* truffle is cream coloured and is the most sought after and expensive. Slightly soft and spongy and round like small potatoes, they taste delicious with an indefinable flavour of caramel. They tell us they are also leaving soon and we plan to meet up later in the year back in South Africa. We tell them when Tom came in from leave, he discovered that a CD that had a photo of a man and a woman standing next to each other had a line drawn through them to 'separate' them. Anthony tells us of a colleague who had an exam to write on the Tuesday so he takes Wednesday, Thursday, Friday and the weekend off to recover. A woman needed to get to her appointment at the hospital and there wasn't anybody around to drive her so she gets her eleven-year-old son to drive. I heard that someone had received a postcard from Italy with a stamp depicting the famous torso of Venus. Apparently this one was wearing an *abaya*! We all chuckle appreciatively at these snippets of life in Saudi. Ah, but what entertainment would there to be had without them.

Victor tells me at teatime that he usually cooks his '*beep in binegar*' to marinade it. He is in chatty mode so I also hear how the fallen Filipino president had a '*pictitious*' name and he had felt very '*prustrated*' as he also had '*pipty-por*' counts of frauds against him. Victor is taking the whole Estrada thing very seriously and watches the impeachment trial fervently every evening. I sip my coffee and nod at the appropriate moments but I am glad when Rehaad comes in to ask me about my leave forms. He tells me, en route to my office, that he hasn't found another wife yet. I tell him he should be glad he has Hannan. He grins and rubs his calloused forehead absently and says he has a pain in his backside. He gathers from my startled expression that he may not have conveyed the correct message and points to his side. He is wrong however. I agree with him that he is a pain in the backside!

Dr. H is looking very smart in his western gear, a charcoal gray suit and blue tie. Grant tells me that they have a name for people like him in the Philippines, 'sip-sip' meaning literally 'seriously person seeking.' Go figure!

"Good morning Janette. Have you reconsidered your leaving us?" asks Dr H hopefully.

I smile at him and give him the same reason as I gave Rehaad. Dr. H knows I'm making a point and sighs.

"I will be leaving for a short vacation soon. I will make sure all your documents and passport are released in time for your departure."

"You have always been so efficient Dr. Hammad" I tell him earnestly. "I will miss that"

He is pleased and tells me,

"I always try to do my but."

I impulsively lean in and give him a quick hug. He tries but fails to look disapproving.

Colin and I are trying to finish everything before we leave. This is proving difficult, as there is so much to do.

He meets me outside Alyssa souq today and as we are walking down the steps outside, a man comes up to us on the steps, and says to me,

"I know you!" I stare at him for a minute; he is short, dark, bearded and is wearing a *thobe and ghutra.*

He holds a clear packet in his hands containing a police uniform.

"I don't know you, I'm sorry." I say politely. He looks at Colin,

"Who are you?" Col looks annoyed and tries to move forward,

"I'm her husband." he says firmly. The man narrows his eyes,

"No, no! She *eez* nurse. She *leev* in Nurse's centre," He jabs his finger behind him and steps closer to Col.

"Well I am her husband. She lives in KWMH compound with me." responds Col trying to push past the man. The man takes a step backwards and speaks angrily,

"I am Mohammed, I am also police. I will report you!"

He shakes the packet containing his police uniform. Col looks down at the packet briefly but remains firm,

"Look, I will show you our marriage certificate," He pulls out his wallet and unwraps a crumpled marriage certificate and thrusts it under his nose. Mohammed looks unimpressed,

"This is not good paper. It is not true." Col has had enough,

"Look, she is my wife. Leave us or I will report *YOU* for harassment!"

This does the trick and the man departs muttering darkly under his breath. We are glad to get home and pour the last of the homemade red.

The Education department has prepared a surprise *masalamah* for me and I am touched. The classroom has been transformed into a farewell feast. A table groans with food, posters are stuck around the room and balloons decorate the windows. I pause in the doorway and see Mercy, Ruth, Jenny, Amelia, Ding, Aster and Grant seated along the window. Even Dr. Who has arrived, Rehaad there too, smiling in his crisp white shirt and pressed pants. Lindy takes me by the hand and leads me over to the table. 'Sit!' she dictates. Grant opens the event with a long flowery speech; Ding gives another little speech followed by Aster and lastly Rehaad, speaking on behalf of Dr. H who is in Amsterdam again. There is a small pile of presents on the table and I am asked to open them all. I have been given brass plates, a leather camel and a beautiful brass hubbly bubbly. I am pleased and taken aback. There is so little money for presents yet they have given willingly for me (at least I hope it was willingly!)

We eat pancetta and vegetables for lunch and the usual assortment of nibbles. The best is a cake that Lindy has had made at Tammimi, that features all the faces of the Education department against a green background of icing. I am again touched and surprised. I wonder how she was able to get a photo of the Muttawa for instance. Later in the morning he also presents me with a present. He watches me shyly as I tear open the paper wrapping. It is a long black abaya dress embroidered with red and gold thread. It is a touching gesture from someone who is supposed to be merely a strict officer of virtue! I have to hide my tears.

Our last week in Saudi is full of farewells. I have another dinner for my *masalamah* from the nursing staff. Leanne is there as well as Anthony the paediatric doctor and the Norwegian Anaesthetist. They have invited Darlene as well. I am presented with a really lovely gift of an ornately carved wooden Arabian mirror window that is closes with ornate wooden shutters. I have often admired them in town. I gaze around at all the nurses and staff that have come to bid me farewell and reflect that really it has been they and the other 'ex pats' we have met who have supported me and made working and living in a strange country more bearable. It strikes me that part of dealing with cultural differences is having them explained along with tried and true ways of dealing with the differences. Most of the people we met did this. Laughter helped diffuse the more unpopular cultural aspects of life. More wine anyone?

Col, Tim and I meet up with Lindy and Len for dinner in the Al-Buhtan hotel. They present us with a painting depicting a Toyota driven by a local with a camel kneeling in the back. It is a typical Saudi scene and I suddenly feel a lump in my throat. Len has brought a plastic bottle of red and we toast each other and enjoy a great meal. Later on I'm horrified to see I'm caught chewing on a piece of gristle in one photo! Most unflattering! The next day I meet up with the head nurses for tea. We stand together for photographs. I bid my last farewell and leave the doors of the education department, King Sayeed Military Hospital, for the last time, waving goodbye and promising to write to everyone . . . 'Ins'Allah'!

EPILOGUE

We DECIDE FOR some reason that may have something to do with a reluctance to return too quickly to the relative 'normality' of home, to leave Saudi Arabia via India and have a three week holiday with eleven pieces of luggage and a nine year old son whose left hand has morphed into a Gameboy. This method of travel is not to be recommended. When we do eventually return to Cape Town we're all suffering from culture shock in reverse. Our house is too small, the shopkeepers I try and bargain with look at me as though I've gone mad, and all the magazines I buy (and I buy a lot!) are strangely denuded of thick black pen scribbles. There is too much female flesh showing. I feel strangely naked without my abaya. We miss the friends we have made and some of the fascinating characters.

Lindy stayed behind for another year before landing herself a job on the ships as a nurse. Delia and I remain good friends to this day. Most of the others stayed for a short while longer before returning home. Those who remain say it's not the same but yet they stay. Colin and I know that the real reason is because after a certain number of years the 'camelisation' process sets in. It is extremely difficult to live anywhere else at this stage. We left just in time.

When our Toyota '*golden jeepbox*' arrives in a container three weeks later, full of the contents of our years in Saudi, the family and I set to unpacking and reliving moments of memory.

I pull out Mo, my stuffed camel and ponder its uniquely supercilious expression fondly.

My brightly coloured cushions and Persian carpets a fond reminder of sitting in Al-Hazim's carpet shop, surrounded by eager assistants who unfurl roll after roll of vibrant carpet while I sit sipping mint tea whilst the thrust and parry of the bargaining process continues to its conclusion.

"You should write about your experiences," suggests mum. I sigh and remove a bright plastic MacDonald's toy from a brass teapot.

"Yes, why don't you mum," says Tim who has found his box of pirated CD games squirreled inside the microwave oven.

"You should write so other women know what to expect if they have to go there," Jo removes my wooden mirror window from a box and wonders whether she could mosaic the side. I wish I had spent more time getting to know the real locals but then, the opportunity did not present itself. I think I met plenty of local characters and many others from foreign lands They had all weaved their way into the tapestry of experiences that made up Saudi Arabia.

"Well, I'll give it a bash." I say unwrapping my old abaya and gazing at it in disbelief, "but I'm not promising anything!"